HOW TO HIRE, MANAGE, AND FIRE YOUR CONTRACTOR

How To Hire, Manage, and Fire Your Contractor

Everything You
Need To Know
To Do It Right

CARMEN AMABILE

HOW TO HIRE, MANAGE, AND FIRE YOUR CONTRACTOR
by Carmen Amabile

LWP Publishing
P.O. Box 66215
Roseville, MI 48066-3795

First Edition 2007, ISBN: 978-0-9793876-2-3
Library of Congress Control Number: 2007901657

This book is dedicated to all homeowners everywhere, and to the professional tradespeople who service their homes.

CONTENTS

GUIDE TO APPENDICES **109**

ACKNOWLEDGEMENTS

The people who influenced me in making this book a reality can go back to my father, who advised me as a teenager to go into my own business. Then I was fortunate to find and fall in love with Kathy, my wife of 29 years, who has supported me in my drive and passion from day one of starting my own business. Many thanks also go to my son and daughter, Paul and Lisa, for their efforts in the family business over the years.

Too many customers to name, the good and bad, helped the system described in this book come to life. Especially, I would like to thank my conscientious customers who took the time to share their desires, needs, problems, suggestions, stories and wants with me. These customers helped teach me the best ways to serve all my clients and helped form the basis of this book project.

Special thanks for their participation, support and feedback go out to Kevin Nolan, Gerry Weinberg, Gordon Burgett (Gordon Burgett Pathfinder Service), Alicia Klein, and Matt Haack.

INTRODUCTION

There is an army consisting of builders, maintenance and alteration contractors, subcontractors and their employees who build and maintain our homes on a daily basis. They tackle jobs we cannot or will not do ourselves. These service providers perform essential or not-so-essential services for us upon our request.

Home construction and maintenance is a multi-billion-dollar industry. This army of workers is important to our own personal infrastructure, maintenance of our homes and our peace of mind. Be it to repair a leaky pipe or build an addition to their home, almost everyone will need to hire a service "contractor" at some time in their lives. When that time comes, you had best be prepared to do battle. The old adage, "In time of peace, prepare for war," rings true. We believe that in the field of home repair, you should prepare for battle to prevent a war.

Home repair consistently ranks in the top three consumer complaints nationally year after year. Consumer fraud in home repair is often in the news. Each report ends with a list of steps that consumers should take to prevent themselves from being ripped off.

Advice includes: get three bids, ask your friends and relatives for referrals, hire licensed contractors, check with the Better Business Bureau and get it in writing.

As often as we hear these suggestions, you can bet that next week or month, you will hear another news account of a "contractor" committing fraud. Why? Because the list of suggestions widely published above is incomplete. It is misleading and it is only the tip of the iceberg in providing homeowners with the necessary information to make an informed and educated decision on whom to hire and whom to invite into their homes.

As a painting contractor for 28 years, I have seen both good and bad service companies in operation. I have observed many frustrated homeowners in their attempts to deal with poor workmanship and failure to perform as well as outright fraud and theft.

This book will provide you with some insight into living with contractors and has been developed over the years as my customers shared their problems with me. Often their problems with their other contractors directly or indirectly affected my work. The skilled trade of painting naturally requires problem-solving ability. The painter's work is performed after all other tradesmen. It is the painter's role to correct and hide any flaws to the best of his ability using the tools of his trade.

Many residential builders do not have painters on their crews for that exact reason. They want to be long gone and cash their check before the homeowner notices all the little flaws.

For example, a homeowner has new windows installed throughout the home. Everything looks fine to the homeowner, the work was completed and she paid the contractor in full. Upon getting an estimate to stain and finish the interior window frames, she discovers that some of the nail heads on the smaller moldings were not counter-sunk. If they are counter-sunk now, due to their positioning, the moldings will crack. She doesn't have any extra pieces of the molding available. The extra costs she willingly paid for the beautiful oak trim so she could have it stained were not enough. It is now going to cost her an additional expense since the mitered corners are poorly cut and need additional work to get them in "ready to stain" condition. She doesn't want the 3/16-inch gaps to be filled in with wood putty, she doesn't like that look. Nor should she have to. She deserves to get what she paid for. The nail holes in the large bay window have been filled in with a white putty, costing additional monies to correct since this putty will not accept the stain uniformly. She is also worried about the deadline; the contractor took two months to complete the job and was to have been finished a month ago. She has tried to contact him to come out and fix a piece of aluminum trim on the exterior windows and he is not returning her calls. To meet her deadline and stay on budget, she gives up and decides to paint the expensive oak trim instead.

Homeowners who heed the insight this book has to offer will greatly increase their chances of getting the job completed to their satisfaction. Law enforcement officials can offer little support once you have been victimized by fraud, misrepresentation and/or poor workmanship by a contractor.

Active support from consumer "watchdog groups" is minimal and can take years before any complaints are acted upon. The elderly and single women are targeted and taken advantage of most often. Steps must be taken by both homeowners and reputable contractors working together to reduce the opportunities and police the environment where unscrupulous contractors can thrive and prey on the unsuspecting homeowner.

Good contractors do exist and they assist homeowners daily,

providing them with high-quality work. Finding these companies is the key to completing a successful project. This book will provide you with the means to finding them and will teach you to monitor their progress as the work is performed. If things go wrong, this book will help you right the course and limit your monetary loss.

Once homeowners are better educated, contractors will need to improve their operations and meet higher standards, helping to draw a more distinct line between "con men" and contractors.

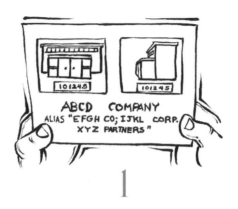

Chapter 1

Choosing Your Contractors

Establish the Plan

So you're planning to remodel your bathroom. You have a budget in mind that you have reached by canvassing friends and relatives who have done similar projects. In your mind, you envision how beautiful it is going to look and how much you will enjoy it. The funds became available since the new financing came through the bank today and you can't wait to get started and have it completed by the end of summer. You've been gathering names of contractors from advertising, word-of-mouth referrals and local trucks driving around the neighborhood. Today you are going to contact them.

The trades required for the project are: plumber, drywall installer, tile layer, electrician, painter and wallpaper installer. You have acquired the names of three tradesmen for each trade along with names of three remodeling companies because your mother told you how much easier it is to hire one company to do all the work. So you start to call the three remodeling companies. Two have answering machines so you leave messages; an employee at the third company tells you that the owner will call you back. So your excitement is put to use and now you begin waiting for the return phone calls. Two of the companies call you back within 48 hours and the third company never calls. You learn it will take a week before they can come out to take measurements and give you a free estimate. So you decide to call the individual tradesmen/contractors on your list. You have 18 names and telephone numbers; four make contact with you and after two weeks of phone tag, you have one estimate and are waiting for two more to arrive by mail. Prices are all over the map and you can't make sense out of all the contradictory information you are getting. Two more weeks pass and you now know that prices have increased and it will cost more than you budgeted. You plan to just keep looking for the right contractors who will do the work at your price because you really want to stay on budget. If you don't stay on budget you know that will have a negative trickle-down effect on all of your plans.

Your Decision

Finally, after a month you decide to go with the contractors that your friend used. The bids you got will keep you on budget and even allow a positive buffer of $500 for any unexpected costs. Fast-forward to the end of the job. Summer is over and your bathroom is almost complete. It has been the worst summer of your life. There were broken promises, contractors not showing up as promised, wrong color sinks delivered and a tile pattern not installed exactly the way you wanted it. The shower pan leaked and ruined your dining room ceiling, on two occasions the contractor's employees showed up intoxicated and you finally stopped trusting them alone in your house. You spent the whole summer at home. You could not wait to get the job completed and all the strange men out of your house. It has not been any fun sharing the half-bath with the workers all summer long. Although there are many female contractors, for the sake of readability, in this book I refer to contractors as he.

Now, the upstairs bathroom is complete and you have been enjoying your new Jacuzzi® bathtub. You have waited two months to have the dining room ceiling repaired just to make sure that the leak caused by the tub was really fixed. The painter informs you that the drywall is bowed and he needs to remove and replace a four-foot by four-foot section of the dining room ceiling. You tell him "OK, just do it right." The painter discovers that the rough carpenter who dismantled your old bathroom cut into your supporting ceiling joist by over 50 percent. The bowed drywall was not due to the water damage but was a sign that your ceiling was collapsing. He advises you to call the city building inspector to verify the situation before he attempts to repair the ceiling.

The city inspector informs you that the painter's assessment was accurate. He advises you to hire a licensed contractor to install an I-beam in your ceiling to prevent the collapse of your ceiling and to stop the bathroom from falling onto your dining room table. He doesn't ask and you don't tell him what contractor did the bathroom remodeling work. You are out of money and the pricing that you are getting for an I-beam is unreasonable as far as you are concerned. You call the contractor who cut out the support joist. He informs you that he has always done it like this in the past and that there has never been a problem. You agree to let him tie into the joist with another joist for support and he promises that this will suffice. You are scared, angry, disillusioned, out of money and you end up with a bathroom that really isn't the way you want it to be. For the next 10 years, every time you hear the floor creak you wonder if the upstairs bathroom is going to fall through your floor.

The Solution

Unfortunately, I have found, and many contractors agree with me, that our best customers are the ones who have been "taken" by at least three other contractors. For some reason it seems that homeowners need many lessons to learn that "You really do get what you pay for." This is especially true if you fail to do your homework and hire legitimate businesses. This means hiring not just tradesmen, not just contractors, but those that are *legitimate businesses*—well run, organized, system-based residential contracting businesses.

> *Choosing which contractor to hire is a financial decision, from selection of the firm to the return on investment.*

So, how do you find good residential contracting service businesses? You will *find them by asking the right questions* and looking for them in the right places. How many friends and relatives do you trust to make sound financial decisions for you? Most people who answer honestly say that they do not look to friends and relatives for advice on money issues. Choosing which contractor to hire is a financial decision. Treat it as if you were deciding which relative you were thinking about letting move into your home and live with you. With whom are you most likely to get along? Which relative would most likely agree to pay you rent on time and obey your house rules? Selecting a good contractor is a very serious decision that can impact your life for quite some time.

This book is about teaching you how to find and manage contractors. Exercise the self-discipline to follow through each step. Avoid putting unnecessary time restraints on your project; these create undue pressure and may cause you to take a short cut in the critical hiring phase of finding a good contractor.

Here is the best way to find a good contractor. If you take a short cut at this stage, it could cost you dearly.

> *Well begun is half done.*
> *—Aristotle*

8 Steps to Hiring a Good Contractor

1. Get Names

Gather the names of up to six contractors from the following sources: print advertisements, supply shops, friends and neighbors, relatives, the Internet, service trucks in your area and lawn signs.

2. Residential and/or Commercial

Find the contractor's advertisements in the yellow pages or other advertising media, including his truck signs, and check to see if he advertises for residential *and* commercial work. *If he advertises for commercial work, you may want to scratch him off your list.* Here is why: commercial work pays more and is more profitable. If time is short, the contractor will always go to a commercial job instead of to your project. Many contractors pile up the residential work at the end of their season only after determining if the commercial side of their business is having a good year or not. That is one reason why you might hear people say, "The contractor never showed up." Another reason you may want to stay away from the commercial contractor is that his crew is geared for maximum production in an environment where *they seldom work for or see the owner of the buildings on which they are working.* They are not well trained in the discipline of working in the privacy of someone's home. On the other hand, a contractor who runs his business exclusively for the homeowner provides the best chance for you to become a satisfied customer.

3. Is He Licensed?

Review his advertisements and see if the contractor states that he is a *licensed contractor.* This assumes that you have done your homework and learned the legal requirements in your state governing residential contractors. In Michigan, any work performed over $600.00 in or on a residential structure requires a licensed contractor. If his advertisements do not say that he is licensed, scratch him off your list. Contractors who have gone and qualified for a license will be happy to let you know about it.

4. Verify the License

Verify licenses for all the contractors on your list and check for complaints filed against them. Many states have a form of a licensing and regulation department at the state level that will field telephone calls from consumers for license verification and complaint history. The Internet is a great source; at many state web sites, you can verify the license online. You can always call the company directly and ask for their license number to make verification easier, especially online. Mark down the following important information once you find a source for verification:

- The full name of the license holder

- The year the license was granted

- The location of the business.

Scratch off your list any contractor whose license cannot be verified or whose license has expired.

5. Is He Insured?

Only hire licensed (if required by law) and insured residential contractors. Check their advertisements to see if they say that they are insured. If so, you will need to verify that the insurance coverage really exists. Many scam contractors advertise only that they are "insured" and leave the word "licensed" out of their ads. "Insured" can mean that the contractor merely has health insurance for himself. This is no joke. I have heard of that exact situation. In another case, the unfortunate homeowner did not find out until after the licensed roofer who painted her kitchen damaged her floor. He advertised licensed and insured, it just wasn't the type of license and insurance that did the homeowner any good (see Chapter 10: Troubleshooting/Leaking Roof for an example of how a roofer could possibly be painting your kitchen).

"Insured" stated in an advertisement can mean the contractor merely has health insurance coverage for himself.

6. Verify Insurance

The best way to verify a contractor's insurance is to call them and ask them to fax you a copy of their insurance "face sheet." You are looking for commercial liability insurance and workers compensation insurance. Now, the contractors on your list that get a call from you asking for proof of insurance have just two ways to think of your request.

1. Contractor A has been sued so many times that he can only suppose that you are looking for a contractor on whom you may attempt an insurance scam.

2. Contractor B is happy to supply the requested proof of insurance because he does good work and is not fearful of a lawsuit. He knows that he can satisfy you and understands that you are a street-smart, seasoned consumer doing your "due diligence" and homework.

What is the value of an estimate when that estimate may be setting you up for failure?

Once you get the proof of insurance, call the listed agent and verify that the insurance policy is still in force and active. Many fraudulent contractors will purchase an insurance policy only to cancel it within 30 days and get a refund less $50. For their trouble, they will have received a face sheet from the insurance carrier saying that they or their company is insured when, in fact, they are not. This type of fraud has become so common that some insurance companies no longer give the "contractor" proof of insurance. These insurance agents tell the "contractor" to have his customers call them to request proof of insurance so that they can fax the paperwork to the contractor's customer directly.

Congratulations, you have just found out who on your list are the best residential contracting businesses! Instead of inviting six complete strangers into your home, you have eliminated some of the obvious liars and cheats and they will not be allowed near you or your family. Job well done, you have just protected yourself and your loved ones in a very responsible way. You have also saved yourself considerable time in waiting around for the liars and cheats to show up for the "Free Estimate," which would enable them to give you an inaccurate bid. This is very important. The bids from unscrupulous contractors would distort your search for a fair price. Their bids are worthless because they really are not in a *business*. Their bids would not reflect the kind of fair price needed to provide you and your loved ones with the necessary protection to reach the goal of a successfully completed job. If the homeowner hires one of these outfits knowing that the contractor is not running a legitimate business, he does so at great peril to his family and his home. Here the homeowner is surely asking for trouble, and the homeowner will surely pay for the trouble.

7. Schedule the Estimate

The next step is to call the residential contractors remaining on your list and schedule an estimate (interview). Do not be discouraged if you have only one company to call out of the six names on your list. Your efforts will pay huge dividends for you in the end.

8. Written Project Description

Write down a precise and clear description of the project for which you require an estimate. For example: "I want you to replace my countertops with Corian® in the kitchen and the powder room" or "I am looking to remodel my bathroom; all the current fixtures will be replaced but the ceramic tile will stay." Memorize the description of your project.

There is a knock on your door and you say to yourself, "What do you know? The guy is on time for the estimate." Now the real fun begins as you determine if this contractor is the one who will help you reach your goal to successfully complete your project.

2

THE ESTIMATE-INTERVIEW

Greet & Meet

You are very well prepared for this encounter. Your attitude of *strictly business* is firmly in place. As you open the door, you remember the old adage "buyer beware." The contractor you have scheduled for this estimate is there at your home because *you invited him*. You need to be sure and remember that this is *your* opportunity to interview the person who wishes to move into your home and perform a professional service for you. This is not just a search for a price. This is the most critical step to successfully completing the project. It is easier to conduct the interview properly and avoid potential litigation; you can fire the contractor right now.

Your guard should be up; you should know more about the contractor than he expects, if you did your research properly and thoroughly. Remember every con man looks his victim in the eye and has a pleasant smile. Do not be fooled.

> *As I grow older*
> *I pay less attention to what men say.*
> *I just watch what they do.*
> *—Andrew Carnegie*

Greet the contractor at the door. Do not offer to shake his hand. Instead, see if he makes the first offer to shake yours. If he does, it demonstrates common courtesy and respect. Look him straight in the eye and notice where he is looking when you open the door to let him in. Do his eyes wander to check out the interior of your house and your belongings or does he look you right in the eye? Does he ignore other family members present in the room? Does he pay too much attention to your spouse and children? Does your pet react to him in the usual manner that your pet normally greets strangers? Be observant. Your observations will form the basis for your decision as to whether you hire his company or not.

Describe the Project

Next, take the contractor to the area of your home in which the work is needed. Recite the project description that you memorized in Step 8. Now, take note of how many times the contractor interrupted you before you could tell him about the project. Don't be surprised if he doesn't interrupt you. This would be a good thing.

Listen Up and Observe

After you describe your project, *you must keep quiet and listen*. Listen to his response. Was he listening to you, was he attentive? Did he seem to understand you? Did he ask for clarification on certain points to make sure that he understood you correctly?

It is very important that you stop talking after you tell the contractor about your project and your needs. If you continue to talk, you will miss important signals that the contractor is sending you. You need to remain quiet and use your eyes and ears at this point in the interview.

Does the contractor take measurements and how is he taking the measurements? Does he use a ruler or a measuring device? Is he walking off the room counting his steps? Some contractors will use the "WAG" system of estimating. In the trades, this is called a "wild ass guess."

Does the contractor ask you questions right away and are they about the project or are they personal? Good contractors will ask you personal questions but they will relate to the project. The contractor will very likely try to determine if you are a serious prospect or if you are just fishing for a price. Most estimates are free to the potential prospect but they are certainly not free to the contractor. He includes the cost of this estimating process in his overhead costs. His time is valuable and he will try to determine right away if you are worth his time.

If the contractor asks questions about the quality of materials you desire, such as granite over Formica®, tell him your true preference. Don't waste his time bidding out granite when you know that the costs are too high for your budget. If he starts to ask you detailed questions about construction matters or how you want the work performed, respond with, "I would like *you* to tell *me* how you would do the project, what materials you recommend and why."

He Talks

Now, remain quiet and listen to his response. Does he do what you asked of him? Is he a good listener? Does he communicate well with you?

Did he tell you how he would do the project or did he just give you more options? If he responds with three different ways to do the project, he demonstrates that he is leaving the choice up to you and you will be responsible for the decision. Listen closely to see if he stands firmly behind his recommendation for how the project should be done. Do not worry about price now. Your focus should be on finding out if this contractor will be able to communicate with you and if he is knowledgeable about his trade(s).

Listen to hear what the contractor willingly tells you about his company and what he *is not* telling you about his company. Does he share with you company policies on safety? Does his company run background checks on employees? Is there a no smoking policy? What about payment schedules, references and professional associations that the company may belong to? Or is he just so focused on you and finding out what he has to do for you in order to get the job that he doesn't offer up any information about himself and the company? Listen closely.

During this interview, you need to discover if the contractor glosses over the process or is he descriptive about the scope of work required. Later you will discover if he places it in writing with a detailed or vague description. He needs to be able to demonstrate a high level of skill both in written and verbal communication, and you need to see it right now, during the interview/estimating process.

He Writes

Some contractors will give you a written proposal during the initial interview, others will mail the proposal to you. After the contractor finishes taking measurements and/or writing up the proposal it will be time for you to ask him more questions.

In this example, we will have the contractor immediately provide you with a written proposal. Be sure to read Chapter 3: Common Mistakes that Homeowners Make, in which we cover many points concerning the estimate gathering process. Look at the contract form and see if his license number is on it. In many locations, license information is required to be on the contract. I call the next set of questions you will ask the Integrity Check.

The Integrity Check

The Integrity Check is a series of questions to which you already know the answer. You are testing to see if this contractor is going to lie to you or if he will demonstrate the integrity of both himself and his company. Ask the contractor how long he has been in business. Your license verification efforts tell you that he has been licensed for five years. If he responds with anything other than five years, he has just set off a red flag. You then ask him who owns the business. The license verification step revealed that his wife's name is listed as the owner. It is fine if someone other than the estimator owns the company. You are just checking to see if the estimator will be honest. If he stutters through your questions, more red flags will appear.

> *Integrity Check: A means to quickly assess*
> *the "character" of a business*
> *you are considering hiring.*

Ask the contractor if he uses subcontractors to perform any or all of the tasks necessary for completion of this job. Most contractors do not want to answer this question and many will launch into a story of how great their crews are and how long they have been working for the company. Persist until he answers your question; the majority of contractors do indeed use subcontractors. If the answer is no, he does not use subcontractors, ask him to put it in writing that he will not use subcontractors on your job. This may provide you with some degree of legal protection if a worker is injured while working on your project. You will also instantly find out if this contractor has any employees on his payroll. If he will not put it in writing, that is OK, don't force him to. Just don't hire him. If he answers that he does use subcontractors, ask him to provide you with written proof of licensing and insurance for all of his subcontractors before he begins working on your project. See Chapter 4: Games that Contractors Play, for more information on subcontractors.

It's Price Time!

Next, look at the price and say, "That is really more than I wanted to spend." Then say, "What is your cash price?" If the contractor drops his price one dollar without reducing labor or material costs, do not do business with him! You are not negotiating to buy a used car here. If the first proposal/option the contractor gave you included an overcharge, what does that tell you about how he does business?

The reason you ask for a cash price is to entrap the unscrupulous contractor. If he drops the price, he just let you know that he wants cash because he cooks his books and he does not report all his income to the government. If he cooks his books, he is most likely paying his workers cash as well. If he is paying his workers cash, he is subcontracting them out. If he is subcontracting out your project, the subcontractors may be able to file liens against your house if the contractor chooses not to pay them. The subs may also be able to file suit against you if they are injured on the job. The subcontractor may have his own "employees" and if they are injured on your job, they may file suit against everyone. If the contractor you hire only uses employees and no subcontractors, the employees cannot sue you for an injury suffered on the job. They are required to go through the Workers Compensation Insurance Fund for lost wages and medical costs.

The contractor you are interviewing should not drop his price without dropping labor or material costs to match. He should be presenting you a price to perform the work at a professional level—a price that will provide you with the successful completion of your project per your description. It is in the contractor's best interest to work with a fine pencil, after all, he has invested his time and resources in you, and he is there to get the job. An established residential service contractor knows his business numbers and knows what he needs to charge to remain in business. He cannot afford to either overcharge or undercharge his customers. The best contractors know their market value, and charge accordingly. The only question is, can you afford him? The contractor knows that *if you don't hire him at his fair market value, someone else will.* The scam contractors who drop their prices for you are not sure if someone else will hire them at the price they need. Instead, they will alter the scope of work or the quality while the job is in progress to meet the numbers they need to be profitable. There are many ways a contractor can play this numbers game, see Chapter 4: Games That Contractors Play.

Is This Your Guy?

So the contractor sitting at your table informs you that he cannot and will not drop the price for cash, it's all the same to him. This is a good thing. This may be your guy. Now, read over the contract closely; make sure that everything is spelled out. Make sure that all of the promises he makes to you are in writing, including:

a) No subcontracting

b) Warranties

c) Guarantees

d) Scheduling

e) Brand and quality of materials to be used

f) Name of carrier for insurance coverage

g) Notice of option to cancel as part of their contract

h) Any special instructions you want him to follow

If everything meets your satisfaction, sign the agreement and give him a deposit if required.

If you need to sleep on it, go ahead, but consumer protection laws allow you to cancel, within three business days, any contract that is solicited in your home for any reason. Check your specific state law. Licensed residential contractors are required to have this notice of cancellation as part of their contract.

Summary

1. You did your homework and verified background information on the contractor.

2. You described the project to him and you kept quiet.

3. You listened and evaluated his communication skills, both verbal and written.

4. You performed the Integrity Check on him and he passed.

No red flags remain but he is your only bid. What do you do? Remember that he knows what he is worth. Think about it. What price would you pay for an honest contractor who can prove his honesty to you? He has faxed you his insurance face sheet. He proves that he took the trouble to comply with state regulations and qualify as a licensed contractor. He demonstrates good communication skills, puts everything in writing and has a clear contract. At this point, if you want to keep looking for another contractor with a better price, go ahead. However, if you can't afford an honest contractor you certainly won't be able to afford a dishonest one.

Price Too High?

When the price is over your budget, you have two options. One, tell the contractor that you want to do business with him but you cannot afford the price. Ask him if he has any suggestions on how the price could decrease without quality suffering. He will appreciate your honesty and will respond with ideas like, "You requested ceramic tile, which is very costly both in terms of material and labor expense. There is a new product that has been on the market for two years that imitates the ceramic tile look but is half the cost. The risk is that if your children or someone else forgets to close the shower curtain properly and too much water sits on the floor, it is likely to warp. Is this something that we should consider?" The second option is to tell the contractor that you will do business with him and you would like to know how long he will honor the price he gave you. Have him put the answer in writing on the contract. Tell him that you need more time to collect the funds and that as soon as you do, you will call him.

In our example, you decide that you can afford to have the project done properly at the contractor's price and you sign him up. Work begins in two months if all the planets align correctly. See Chapter 5: Understanding Contractors for some of the ways that the situation can get out of alignment.

> *If homeowners are unwilling to do their homework, giving a deposit to a contractor will be more of a gamble than it need be.*

3

COMMON MISTAKES THAT HOMEOWNERS MAKE

Dos and Don'ts of Customer Behavior

Many problems that homeowners have in getting quality work from residential service contractors are caused by the homeowner's lack of knowledge on the "Dos and Don'ts" of customer behavior. Awareness of common mistakes and how to avoid them is critical in reaching the goal of a successfully completed project.

Is the customer, really, always right? Not if they do any of the following when hiring a contractor.

1. **Don't do all the talking about how and what you want done during the estimate.**

   State your project goal, then be quiet and *listen*. The estimator/salesman is trained to get you to talk so he can discover your "hot button" and then make the sale.

2. Don't interrupt the contractor as he provides information about his company and methods of operation.

Listen closely to his description of his company or the company that employs him. Hear what he *isn't* talking about. Pursue information about any items that are vague or unclear.

3. Don't tell the contractor that you are living alone (if you are widowed, divorced, etc.).

Your private affairs need to remain private. Human nature being what it is, you need to protect yourself from bias, prejudices and stereotypes. Be all business: *strictly business.*

> *The most valuable of all talents is*
> *that of never using two words when one will do.*
> *—Thomas Jefferson*

4. Don't mention more than once that price is an issue in determining who gets the work.

The estimator will hear you loud and clear the first time. Making price the main issue turns this into your "hot button" for the estimator and he may withhold information/choices from you to keep costs down.

5. Don't describe how other contractors have cheated you.

Chances are he won't feel sorry for you. In residential service there is plenty of truth to the cliché "You get what you pay for." He might even think that you are an easy mark because you're telling him the scams of which you are aware. Therefore, he'll be sure to use a new one on you.

6. Don't supply the contractor with the materials to do the work.

When you supply materials, you provide the contractor with a viable excuse to blame you when things go wrong on the job. After all, you provided the flawed material, not him.

7. Don't offer food and drinks to workers in the morning.

Remember this is a business transaction. Greeting workers in the morning with coffee and donuts sends the common message that the homeowner wants the workers to like them. Many homeowners think this will help them get a better job from the contractor's employees. In fact, when you feed the contractor's employees in the morning you are slowing down production. At some point on your job, the foreman will see the loss of time and pressure employees to hurry up and complete the project. Rushing the workers is detrimental to the successful completion of the job and the overall quality. If you consider the offering of food and drink to be a common courtesy, then ask the contractor or his foreman when the crew's scheduled breaks are and make your offer of food and drinks at that time. This technique will earn the respect of your contractor and again send the message that you are *all business*. Otherwise, you risk sending the message that you are a "softy."

8. Do not give direct criticism of work quality to workers.

Be patient and be tactful. Most people do not possess good communication skills. Most of us are not bosses with the experience to discipline employees. Nobody likes criticism. Leave this unpleasant task to the contractor/foreman. Give him the chance to assign blame and take responsibility for the crew's performance and morale.

9. Don't tell the contractor your occupation.

What he *doesn't* know about you is to *your* benefit. Again, avoid triggering the contractor's biases and prejudices. All the contractor needs to know is your goal for him and that he is in a business transaction with you.

10. Don't reveal if you have sued contractors in the past.

Telling the contractor about problems with past contractors is the fastest way to get an additional "risk" charge passed on to your bottom line.

11. Don't over-schedule estimates so that contractors will meet each other.

This is rude and disrespectful of the contractor's time. It is not uncommon for the contractors to get together to compare notes and add an extra dollar amount. At least one of them will benefit from the inconvenience.

12. Don't miss the timely payments you agreed to when you signed the contract.

Not paying on time sends the wrong message to the contractor. You increase his stress on the job. You motivate him to qualify you as a potential problem customer. Don't provide him with an excuse to withdraw from the job or to justify his lack of production and/or reduction in quality.

13. Don't succumb to pressure from a contractor to make more payments or larger payments than what was originally agreed upon.

Strictly business is your motto. Stick to the terms of the written contract in every aspect unless you have agreed upon and signed written Change Orders. Contractors who ask for more money have failed to get the message that you are "all business" and that you expect him to be "all business" as well. If a contractor asks for more money before a scheduled payment is due, this is a sign of trouble on the horizon.

14. Don't put excessive pressure on the contractor to finish the job.

Putting pressure on the contractor is a quick way for the contractor to justify rushing the workers, lowering quality and crew morale. This will result in you paying *more* for *less* than is called for by the original contract.

15. Don't wait to inspect work until the final day.

Your responsibility is to inspect the daily progress of the work. You negotiated and signed the contract, so you must closely monitor the job site.

16. Don't hand the contractor a checklist of flaws when he expects the final payment.

This tactic of presenting a checklist at the end is unfair and puts everyone at a disadvantage. It is unfair because you failed to previously identify areas of concern to the contractor and he operated under the premise that you were satisfied while the work was ongoing. It is to the customer's disadvantage because the now angry contractor may do minor touch ups to save his profit and attempt to wear you down by claiming to fix your checklist items. This happens all the time. If he tells you that he has fixed xyz, you check it and find it unsatisfactory. He fixes it again, on and on until you finally give up and pay him off just to get him out of your life.

25

17. Don't talk to workers when they should be working.

Distractions lead to accidents, lost productivity, increased job costs and angry foremen/contractors.

18. Don't share personal problems with the contractor.

Keep it all business, strictly business; any personal information given may be used against you.

19. Don't imply that if the contractor does a really good job, you have more work and all sorts of friends who will hire him.

This is an old tactic still in use by homeowners to bribe their contractor. The contractor will eventually see through this if you do not deliver and he could resent that you didn't follow up. Therefore, you either lied to him or no matter how hard he works or how good the quality of his work, he will feel that you cannot be satisfied or trusted.

20. Don't change the original contract if at all possible.

Avoiding changes keeps things simple. No changes mean no add-on charges. If you do change the contract, you position yourself to accept the price as stated by the contractor without going through any bid process. This may work, but only if you hired well in the first place.

21. Don't quote from a do-it-yourself manual as to how the contractor is doing the work incorrectly.

Placing your trust in a do-it-yourself manual over the contractor's job experience is a sure way to pay premium add-on costs and never get this company back into your home to service warranty work.

22. Don't assume that the work is completed before the contractor informs you that it is.

Too many times homeowners inspect the work after the crew has left for the day and assume the worst if any item appears to be poorly installed. They may call the contractor's office, leaving an angry or tense voice mail, only to learn the contractor knows about the problem and is already working to correct it. Inspecting the work is the right thing to do. Assuming the worst—thinking the contractor is done and is planning to leave it that way—will upset many homeowners. Stay calm don't assume the worst.

23. Don't accuse the contractor or workers of personal property damage without proof.

Accusations that are false in the minds of workers and contractors can sour the whole job and will affect the morale of the crew.

24. Do not hover over workers' shoulders while they perform the job.

Many employees get nervous when they feel that their every move is being watched. Check in on them but give them plenty of space so that they can provide maximum productivity and quality.

25. Do not pit workers against the contractor.

Good employees tell their boss how the customer is treating both them and the company. I've had customers offer alcohol to my painters on the job, cash on the side to do small add-on jobs on the clock, and large side jobs to be performed for cash on the weekends.

27

26. Don't approach the workers with offers for cash side jobs.

If you violate the trust of the business relationship, both the employee and the contractor will take steps to protect themselves. This is disrespectful and potentially destructive to your relationship with the contractor.

27. Don't tolerate any solicitation from employees.

Inform the contractor immediately. Most contractors have a strict company policy against this behavior. Employees who solicit anything from you will have broken the company rules. It serves your best interest in two ways to inform the owner/contractor: 1. You are keeping to the "strictly business" approach and letting everyone know about it. 2. You build trust with the contractor. The fact that you discreetly tell him about a problem lets him know that you care about his business.

28. Don't write checks with insufficient funds available.

Keep to the schedule of payments agreed to in the contract. These payments are very important to the small business owner with cash flow concerns. This is the most important role you have in the eyes of the contractor.

29. Don't cause delays in production with personal issues.

Issues such as doctor appointments, pets or children causing damage make more work for the contractor. If you cause obvious delays or damage resulting in additional labor, speak up and tell the contractor that you will cover the additional charges needed to correct the problem. Doing so will qualify you as a valued customer who has earned the respect of the contractor. You will stand out among his good customers.

30. Do not tolerate rude, crude or abusive language or activities on the job site.

If the foreman is on-site, pull him off to the side and let him know specifically what behavior needs to stop. If the foreman is not on-site, either tell him when he returns or promptly contact the contractor.

31. Do not neglect your responsibility to have the job site ready for the arrival of the workers every morning.

Be appropriately dressed; if you moved any of the crew's belongings, be sure they are put back as they were the night before. Remove any personal items from the work zone that might have crept back into the wrong place and make yourself available to answer any questions.

32. Do not raise your voice or get emotional when things go wrong.

Stay professional, *especially* when things are going wrong. This is your best chance to correct the problems and straighten out the issues, getting everyone back on course. If your personality is one that struggles with this type of self-control, put everything in writing and hand the letter to the contractor.

33. Do not hire contractors based on your prejudices, biases and stereotypes.

If you do, the contractor will notice and can use it against you. For example, you hire a contractor because he is "(enter your own ethnic group here)." In your conversation with him you mention that one reason you hired him is "(enter your own ethnic group here) are such hard workers." Things start to go wrong on the job and you approach the contractor on certain issues, his response is "You know us (enter your own ethnic group here) are hard working and we are working hard for you. You must also know that (enter your own ethnic group here) don't like to be told what or how to do the work either."

> *DO NOT hire your next contractor using your normal consumer purchasing habits.*

34. Don't hire contractors on an emotional basis.

Emotions play a major role in making consumer purchases. Consumer purchases of consumable goods and man-made products like automobiles, computers and the like are influenced by our emotions and feelings. Advertisers invest billions to brand their products to reach the individual on an emotional plane. Impulse buying means an emotional purchase that you make right here, right now. DO NOT hire your next contractor using your normal consumer purchasing habits. Your emotional response and feelings toward the contractor should only be 25% of your decision. The other 75% of the decision should rely on reason and logic to determine who is hired. Hiring contractors is not the sort of purchase you are accustomed to making. You are purchasing the time and skills of a real human being. The purchase of time belonging to a human brings into the equation the feelings, reason and logic of the human who is being hired. Imagine if your automobile or toaster had feelings that you had to deal with every time you had to use it. For a more detailed discussion of this topic, see Chapter 5: Understanding Contractors.

35. Do not take things personally.

The work being done is in your private home. Not all things are equal to you here. This is YOUR castle! Everything about this work environment means an emotional attachment for you. You need to be mindful of the *"strictly business"* attitude to pull you through to the successful completion of your project. If an employee of the contractor accidentally breaks your favorite vase, you need to respond like a store merchant. The shopkeeper must decide if he will make you pay for the damage of a broken vase or just clean it up and take the loss because he wants you to continue shopping in his store, today and always, and with a good attitude.

36. Do not approve add-ons *without requiring proof of need.*

Get explanations from the contractor as to why he missed specific add-ons in the estimating phase. This technique brings into play a checks and balances approach to containing cost overruns. It also will give notice to the contractor that you do not have an open checkbook at his disposal.

37. Do not give verbal add-on approvals.

Contracts in use today address the "Change Order" or add-on issue in one of two ways.

1. All changes must be in writing.
2. All additional labor not listed in the contract will be performed at an additional charge.

The second clause is used because too often customers will delay or not make themselves available to sign Change Order forms in a timely fashion. Some consumers will purposely avoid signing Change Orders and refuse to pay for them when the final bill comes due. Either way, whether your contract requires written approval for add-ons, you should get a written description of the add-on work along with the additional charges. Make sure that both you and the contractor sign it before the work begins. If the contractor is reluctant to put the change in writing, do it yourself.

38. Don't share information between contractors.

When a contractor tells you that he is going to do this or that and recommends that the work be performed in a certain way, do not ask the other contractors/bidders what they think of the idea. Do not ask contractors if they plan to do the same thing as the other bidders. Your goal is to listen and to find out what each contractor naturally brings to the job as an individual.

Summary

If a service contractor or his employees take advantage of you in your own home, it creates long-lasting resentment and a bitter taste. Some people have actually come to hate their homes because of it. Your very peace of mind is at stake, and it carries a high price. Take responsibility for your important role in the successful completion of your projects by avoiding the common but serious mistakes listed in this chapter.

Now that you have a clearer vision of the role of a home-owner, let's look into what makes contractors click and how to better understand them.

The quality of an individual is reflected in the standards they set for themselves.
— Ray Kroc

4

GAMES THAT
CONTRACTORS PLAY

In this chapter, when we use the term *game* we mean strategic positioning by the contractor that will benefit himself or his company. This unfairly biases the contract in the contractor's favor, which puts the consumer at a disadvantage.

Deposits

When a deposit is paid to a contractor, the transaction becomes legal. Without the exchange of value, the contract does not have the same legal standing under the law. Once monies exchange hands, protections under the law take effect, guarding the rights of both parties.

One game a contractor may play is not requiring a deposit so the homeowner's rights under the law are not activated. This benefits the contractor who wants the option to back out of the deal if 1. A better deal comes along where he can make even more money; 2. He intentionally overbooks his schedule and then chooses the most profitable jobs to perform. So the home-owner thinks he has a signed agreement with a start or completion date on it. He believes he finally found a good contractor who will perform the work within the budget and complete the project on time. In reality, all the homeowner has is hope outlined on a piece of paper. The contractor can walk away from this deal without any penalty since nothing of value was exchanged. Delays in starting a job or failure to meet deadlines can become very costly to homeowners.

> *In reality, all the homeowner has is*
> *hope outlined on a piece of paper.*

Imagine if the homeowner had a deadline and the foundation work fell behind schedule, causing a ripple effect of delays. The homeowner may incur additional costs for such delays. The homeowner will be under immense pressure to find another contractor to complete the project.

If the delays multiply, as they inevitably will, and force the roof installation into bad weather months, you might lose your roofer. That reputable roofer you had found is forced to alter his schedule and he decides that he can't service your project. You can bet that all of the reputable roofing companies will be booked solid at that time of year and the homeowner will most likely end up with a problem contractor or sub-quality workmanship to meet the deadline. All of this can happen, thanks to the seemingly trustworthy contractor who didn't require a deposit. Do you see how the game is played?

Vague Terms

If you contract a painter to paint your bedroom and he writes up the contract stating, "paint bedroom," you are signing up to play a game once he starts. Here's how. Depending on the color currently on your walls and the new color you want on your walls you may need one to three coats of paint for complete coverage. Contractors play this game to modify the terms once the crew has started the project and after you have accepted his low price. This game is called "low-balling."

The contractor will blame the color selection for the add-on charges and you have no way of knowing if he charged you for one coat, two coats, or three coats in his original bid. If you disagree, he may walk off the job and will most likely overcharge you for the work he has performed.

Low-Balling: A contractor presents a low price with vague terms to get the job, only to raise the costs after the project begins.

Vague terms, descriptions, responsibilities, payment plans, etc. will lead to confusion even if you hire a reliable and trustworthy contractor. Have the agreement written in such a way that months from now, a third party will be able to understand the scope of work and you will avoid the game of "low-balling."

Materials Switch

Suppose you hire a contractor because he sold you on his knowledge of his trade and the products he plans to install and use on your project. For example, you were impressed with his overall knowledge of the construction of replacement windows and the difference between offerings from the national manufacturers. He lists on his contract that he will be using a specific manufacturer of windows or paint. What you may not know is that the manufacturer produces a similar line of windows or paint and puts the manufacturer's label on it. Most people will never recognize that it is not the company's top-line product. National paint manufacturers produce anywhere from three to five different lines of paint. Which did your painter write down that he would be using, the $8 per gallon paint or the $50 per gallon paint?

One homeowner that I knew came home to find all of the custom-made windows for his home delivered and stacked in his garage. To his surprise, all the window manufacturer labels had been removed down to the label adhesive. When he inquired as to where the labels were and asked for proof that the windows were of the specific quality and from the same manufacturer as stated in the contract, the contractor stalled his answers. To the homeowner's dismay, the windows were installed one day before he was to get proof from the contractor as to their source of manufacture. A subcontractor who claimed ignorance as to the issue of quality and source of manufacture installed them. This issue was never rectified and the homeowner had to settle for less expensive windows than those he paid for and justifiably expected. The contractor won this game and surely laughed all the way to the bank.

Subcontracting

Homeowners, more times than not, buy at low to middle prices just to play it safe. Contractors know this. The game that contractors play by using subcontractors is the game of "plausible denial." This all starts with the Internal Revenue Service.

An employee, as defined by the IRS, is essentially a person who is told what to do, when to do it and how to do it. Contractors work with their staff in two ways: hire them as employees or subcontractors. A contractor may actually use both in some cases.

Contractors can offer lower prices when they use subcontractors instead of employees. They circumvent the law, placing all the risk with the homeowner and the technician performing the task. How? The subcontractor may or may not sign an "independent contractor agreement" with the contractor. In this agreement, the subcontractor agrees to carry his own liability and workers compensation insurance. If no agreement is used, and most of the time this is the case, the contractor pays the sub/employee with a check with no deductions made for taxes. The contractor then files a 1099 Miscellaneous Income statement for the subcontractor at the end of the year. Many times the technicians aren't aware that they will need to pay taxes until January 31st of the following year. If the subcontractor is paid cash and signs a receipt for the cash, the contractor has proof of payment and the same applies with filing the Form 1099. The contractor will want minimum written proof to protect himself when things go wrong. Most homeowners will not be aware of this arrangement and will only find out its importance when things go wrong on the job.

The game of plausible denial comes into play when the technician is injured and files a lawsuit against the homeowner since he is not covered by workers compensation. Your contractor will then inform you that his insurance doesn't cover "other businesses." He will also use this excuse if property damage occurs to your home. He will refuse to file a claim against his liability insurance policy, claiming the subcontractor's insurance company should be the one covering your loss and, by the way, that subcontractor is now out of business. The same holds true for warranty protection issues. The contractor you hired will take the position that he also is the victim of a fraudulent contractor since he trusted the subcontractor. A contractor can use multiple layers of subcontractors as "employees" to fulfill the contract and to protect himself and his company from the homeowner.

> *The use of subcontractors allows some service companies to offer the homeowner a lower price (smaller investment). With the lower price comes higher risks passed onto the homeowner, putting their return on investment in jeopardy.*

Wait, it gets worse for the homeowner. Suppliers can file liens against your home if the subcontractors do not pay for the materials they have used on your job. Subcontractors are companies that show up to service your project. These are companies you did not choose and are not sure whether you even want them around your family or home. Subcontractors provide a built-in excuse for all the problems that the contractor may face. For this layer of protection the contractor will pass on all the risk to you, and they will charge you a markup.

Even the legitimate "general contractor" companies using good subcontractors will benefit with the "plausible denial" excuse at a cost to you. It's called a mark-up, usually at a minimum of 10% and as high as 25%. This is 10% over the cost of what it actually takes to get a reliable tradesman to your home. The reliable tradesman knows his market value and will work for only a fair hourly rate. Either you will pay a premium price to the "general contractor" who marks up his profit margin or the general contractor will have to find below-average tradesmen who work and perform for less per hour to remain price competitive. Thus, subcontractors allow the playing of this game where the contractor wins in many different ways. Homeowners who contract with a company that uses subcontractors put themselves at risk and expose themselves to major problems right from the start, before any work begins.

In the commercial and industrial markets, all general contractors and their "subs" must put up performance bonds on many projects for the protection of the contracting party. What does the commercial marketplace know that the residential marketplace doesn't know? Homeowners need to evaluate the value to risk ratio when choosing to do business with any company that uses subcontractors. Assume that the contractor uses them unless they tell you:

1. Their company policy is *not* to use them.

2. They put it in writing for you.

3. They bring up the topic *without you mentioning it.*

If your project is so big that you have no choice but to choose a company that uses subcontractors, do the following. Have the company supply you with proof of licensing and insurance for all subcontractors. Inquire into how long the contractor has been using his subcontractors. Ask him for the names of his best subcontractors for each trade. Insist that he puts in writing that those specific subcontractors will be doing your work. Do not pay the final payment until your contractor has provided you with a Wavier of Lien signed by all subcontractors.

Blame

The blame game is played by the contractor to alleviate himself of the responsibility for the results. The contractor will design his organization, regardless of size, to put the company outside the realm of total responsibility. One example is a remodeling contractor that does not offer painting and decorating services. The painter/decorator will be applying the primer and paint that will display the good *and* bad workmanship of the rough carpenter, the finish carpenter and the drywall installers. The general contractor or remodeling contractor is long gone when the homeowner discovers the sub-standard workmanship. This is the reason that they do not have a painting crew.

Contractors make a conscious decision not to perform certain services that are directly related to the work conducted and the problem-solving nature of the maintenance and/or repairs. For example, the roofer who does not install eaves and downspouts distances himself from blame if the roof leaks around the outer edges. He will tell you that the leak is caused by the way the eaves were installed or that there are not enough downspouts for the water that comes off of the roof. When you call your gutter installer, he blames the roofer because he did not correctly install a roof drip edge, ice shield or valleys. Likewise, your gutter company does not install roofs either. It is a great game for the contractor because the chances are good that he can find another contractor to blame. Perhaps he can even blame you for a do-it-yourself money-saving step that you took upon yourself to try to stay within budget, for example supplying your own materials. The contractor may say something like, "The 15-year shingle you purchased on sale really was of poor quality. I didn't say anything when you had me install it because I thought that you knew what you were doing when you selected that product."

Another example of the blame game occurs with paint and plaster/drywall problem areas. The painting company will not repair plaster or drywall and likewise, the plaster or drywall companies will never paint. If the water repair area that both worked on peels again they will blame each other or even the plumber or roofer. The company that was to stop the water from penetrating your interior walls will blame both the painter and the plaster repair companies. It is like a game of hot potato. You bounce the blame all around until the homeowner gets tired of playing and moves on.

Intimidation

This game is the most distasteful of them all. I have heard of this one being used against the elderly, young couples and single women living alone. The contractor or the employees start to make the customer feel uncomfortable in their own homes once the contractor determines that the customer is unreasonable, difficult to work with or too picky. He may be unhappy that the customer won't give advance payments upon request, is too demanding or a truckload of other whims, biases and prejudices of the contractor or his employees. This game begins when the contractor or his employees/subs start to raise their voices to you, use foul language or walk off the job without telling you when they plan on returning. They may start to tell you stories about threats made to other customers like you who did not change their behavior, or describe what the contractor did when the last homeowner did not pay. The result is to get you to pay as much as 90% of the cost while you are receiving less than

90% of the services required in the contract. They may also try to persuade you to change the payment schedule. Most of their victims will write the check or settle without resolving the issues just to get the contractor out of their lives. As if this isn't bad enough, the homeowner will often keep such intimidation a secret out of embarrassment. This leaves the contractor free to continue working in their neighborhood and advertising in their local paper with no one the wiser.

If this is happening to you, get help with this contractor immediately. Depending on your situation, you can choose to have a forceful friend, an attorney, your son, daughter, the building inspector or your neighbor present when you have your next meeting with the contractor. Let the contractor know that you are not alone and remind him by having witnesses that he had better be careful how he chooses to conduct himself.

Warranties

The game played with warranties is common. Typically, the consumer does not get to see or read warranties until the work is completed or the product installed. The warranty is offered as a major incentive for purchasing the product or service in the initial stage of hiring the contractor. These are warranties such as: "Never paint again," "Maintenance free," "50-year warranty," or "Guaranteed for as long as you own your home." Some of the more comical instances occur when the contractor offers a warranty for longer than he has been in business. Of course, any lifetime warranty begs the question, whose lifetime: yours, mine or the life of the product?

Most of the warranties covering products are from the manufacturers. These warranties seldom cover the labor cost for replacement or re-installation. For example, in the paint industry, a leading manufacturer introduced a new product with a 50-year warranty. After two years of marketing the 50-year warranty, the manufacturer had significant claims of product failure. When a claimant came in, they would simply hand the homeowner a quart of paint for touching up the failed coating. In the third year of marketing the product, they changed the warranty to "for as long as you live in the home." On average, most Americans change homes every five years, so that is a considerable drop in performance guarantee—from fifty years to five.

Labor warranties are tough to get, as most companies are not that confident in their employees. When you receive a warranty that covers all of the labor performed, you actually do have a warranty with value.

Ask for a copy of all warranties prior to the installation of products and/or the signing of the contract. Read them and assign them a value to assist you in the decision-making process.

When aluminum siding entered the market in the mid to late sixties, it was marketed as maintenance-free, "Never paint again." Fifteen years later the factory-painted finish was washing down onto the brick facade and defacing the brickwork on many homes. The cat was out of the bag, and the overselling of "Maintenance-free" became all too well known in the marketplace. The "Tin Men" and the manufacturers did not disappear. Instead, they created a new product to pitch the same way as "Maintenance-free"—vinyl siding. To correct the aluminum siding paint chalking issue, they began telling the consumer that the color was now impregnated throughout their product. If you read a manufacturer warranty on vinyl siding, most do not cover fading, chalking and discoloration of the finished look. These are the same escape clauses that exist for warranties on aluminum siding. This escape clause also exists on replacement windows clad in vinyl or aluminum. So, if you think you are buying a product or surface that is going to save you time and money by being maintenance-free, insist on a copy of the warranty first for verification of the contractor's claim. Do not ever play the game of warranty with your contractor. Remember all warranties are null and void if the installation of the product is not followed exactly as directed by the manufacturer. Additionally, warranties seldom, if ever, cover labor charges.

Summary

When you buy a board game from the store, you open it and have all the pieces needed to play the game. When you plan to hire out a residential service project, your home is the game board, and the game instructions are your written contract. The play money is the real money in your checking account. The game pieces are now real human beings: homeowner, spouse, children, pets, contractor, office employees, subcontractors, employees and suppliers. The goal of the game should be to complete your project in a timely manner with professional results at a reasonable cost to you, the homeowner, with all players achieving their goals. Ultimately, this game should be played with a goal of win-win for all parties involved.

However, as when playing board games, not all players choose to play fair, nor are they interested in you winning. They tend to focus solely on their own needs and desires. In Chapter 9, we will look at the games homeowners play.

5

UNDERSTANDING
CONTRACTORS

All service companies, from the one-person shop to the large-service franchise companies, are in the business of selling their time. Regardless of their trade, each company exists to earn a living and a profit. Then why do some of these companies fail to provide even basic services to their customers?

Why are telephone calls not returned, appointments not kept, deadlines not met, nor lines of communication kept open with you? It makes no sense to the consumer, who is baffled by this behavior from the very people who are in business to serve them. Perhaps if homeowners understood the job requirements of contracting, they would be better able to assess which contractors are the good ones.

Contractor Job Description

1. Able to communicate verbally and in writing
2. Knowledgeable in and able to apply:
   a. Time management skills
   b. Accurate estimating skills
   c. Execution of on-site job safety programs
   d. Multitasking ability
   e. Personnel management
   f. Leadership
   g. Knowledge of the trade
   h. Knowledge of trade standards and building code requirements
3. Self-motivated
4. Motivator of others
5. Good listening skills
6. Project management abilities
7. Accessible/easy to contact
8. Resourceful
9. Sets a high standard of salesmanship
10. Able to monitor market conditions
11. Able to monitor new laws governing the trade and business
12. Able to monitor innovations and products
13. Meets government regulations
14. Expert in crisis management
15. Teacher and trainer of the trades
16. Patient
17. Trustworthy

The Skills

Many skills are required to make a living in residential contracting. Often contractors go out of business because they do not meet the job description listed above. During the interview you can determine if this contractor has what it takes to help you complete your project successfully. How many people have you interviewed? How good are *your* listening and communication skills? Don't worry, by the time you finish reading this book, you will know more about contractors and the business of contracting than the average contractor.

Many residential contractors are contractors by default. They did not go into business with any type of business plan or forethought. Some started their contracting business because they were laid off from their previous job and they will go back to that other job as soon as the economy recovers. Some were fired from a contracting firm that gave up on training them.

> *The first change you need to make is in your*
> *understanding of what a business really is,*
> *and what it takes to make one work.*
> —*Michael E. Gerber*, **The E Myth, Why Most Small**
> **Businesses Don't Work And What To Do About It**

Imagine finding a contractor who meets the job description above. Now add on all the skills needed to perform the physical task of performing the trades: carpentry, plumbing, electrical, plastering, painting, wallpapering, roofing or flooring. This is the impossible challenge faced by a one-man shop. Do you wonder why, at some point, the owner/tradesman could fail to meet your expectations? He is simply over-loaded. If he does not leave your job site during the day to perform estimates, he is working long hours into the night performing estimates for his next job. The chain reaction of the contractor dropping the ball on one of his responsibilities can and will affect the quality of work and service you will receive. Compound the contractor's problem with a homeowner who is difficult to please and prone to making a number of the common mistakes listed in Chapter 3 and you have a glimpse into the enormity of the problem.

Broken Promises

General contractors, remodeling companies, or the two-man or larger shops have another problem: broken promises. If one employee fails to show up for work, the trickle-down effect can be disastrous for both the homeowner and the contractor. If supplies do not arrive on time, job performance lags behind. If the weather does not cooperate or the customer accidentally locks out the crew while hastily leaving the house, promises made by the contractor can be broken. Many times, at no fault of the contractor, but because of third parties, including customers, promises will be broken. *If you lack understanding of the nature of the contracting business, in no time at all, you will find fault with your contractor.* Even the one-man shop will have a problem when add-on work accumulates, making him two weeks late for the start of another customer who only hired him because he said he could complete the project before a certain date.

This recalls the stage performers who spin multiple plates on thin poles. Usually they have six or more plates going at once; they start out one plate at a time, spinning slowly, and then keep adding more poles and plates. When the performer has all his plates spinning, he appeals to the crowd and is awarded with a nice round of applause. Then, right on cue, the first plate starts to wobble and the performer rushes to grab the pole and keeps it spinning. Now the real show begins as the performer skillfully keeps all of the plates spinning to the delight of the crowd as he performs his laughable antics, making sure he keeps the poles spinning without breaking any plates. He wraps up his performance with a perfectly executed dismounting of all the plates. Regardless of the size of the contracting business you may hire, if you do not do your homework and interview well, hire well, listen carefully, avoid common mistakes or keep your end of the contract, your project will be one of the plates that come crashing to the ground.

Skilled Labor

If a consumer behaves in a professional manner toward a contractor and his employees throughout the project, he will dramatically increase the odds of successfully completing the project.

In the residential service market, much of the cost is labor. Physically *skilled* labor comes with a high price tag. Training an individual in any trade is risky. It is a necessity, but also a risk to the contractor. During economic boom years, many good employees will branch off into their own contracting businesses, leaving their employers short-handed and needing to find and train other workers. Imagine the problems faced by a contractor starting a job when his key personnel have just walked away. Often the owner/contractor ends up performing the work himself or is forced to subcontract that portion of the job out to another company or individual. Quality suffers throughout the project or at the very least, the contractor is working overtime to protect his customer and his own reputation. Recovering from the loss of a well-trained employee places a dangerous strain on company resources.

A good employee does not always make a good contractor. Shortly after starting on his own, the employee finds that the multiple hats he must wear do not fit him all that well. It might take that employee two years to discover, if indeed he ever does, that instead of reaching his goal of making more money per hour he actually is making less. *His learning curve will cost you dearly if you hire him.*

You will replace the contractor who incurred the costs to train and develop this man into a tradesman. Many employees leave a good contractor because they are tired of taking orders from a boss who "does everything wrong anyway." This type of worker will not tend to listen to you and you should not be surprised if he tells you you're not his boss.

Employee training is a major issue for every successful residential contracting company. Any trade school that exists mainly feeds the larger commercial and industrial trade companies. Why? Those jobs pay higher wages and generally are union jobs with better benefit programs than the smaller residential companies offer. The residential contracting labor pool is in a crisis and next in line is the commercial contracting labor pool. Estimates suggest that up to 50% of the available labor force has an alcohol or drug abuse problem. Ex-convicts learn the trades in the prison system and the government often provides employers with tax credits of up to 35% of their first year's wages if the company hires former inmates. If you are just out of prison and can't find a good job working with a large firm because they can and do perform background checks, where can you go for employment? You guessed it! Residential service contractors.

This recently-released individual can also choose to start up his own business. *No checks and balances protect the homeowners like the checks and balances in place at larger companies.* The money, manpower and political pressure does not exist. You are on your own and you had best be prepared to protect yourself and your family by investing in a good contractor.

Word-of-Mouth

Another aspect of residential service contracting that homeowners do not understand is the phenomenon of word-of-mouth. Homeowners put too much stock in word-of-mouth referrals and are encouraged to do so by some consumer advisory bodies. You know the drill: check with your friends, relatives and neighbors. Do you really think that they are having different results than you and everyone else? How many people do you know who go out of their way at parties to tell you of a bad choice they made in hiring a contractor or any other embarrassing decision? Yes, I know that angry consumers will trash a company's name or product and that it can have an impact on the company. However, for the most part in the residential service market, word-of-mouth does not make or break a contractor. Think about it. If word-of-mouth were such a powerful tool for accountability, it would be putting contractors out of business daily. It doesn't. Bad contractors move on to their next victim with impunity and only disappear from the residential service market when they decide to.

Word-of-mouth is overrated when it comes to the residential service market. This is because the person trashing the contractor has a reputation in the community and within their circles of friends. Let me explain. When I provide a referral list to my prospective customers, some will recognize the names of friends and acquaintances on the list. I hear comments such as, "If you can please Mr. Jones, you can please me, he is so picky," or, "Is that Dr. Smith's wife? She is something else." When someone trashes a contractor they have hired, people who know them think the problem must be partly the person telling the story. This also holds true in the court system. The consumer is hardly ever found to be entirely without responsibility as to the cause and effect of the problems with a contractor or with the outcome of the project. The reason is that the consumer was not forced into hiring the contractor in the first place.

I grew up in the Detroit, Michigan metropolitan area; over 4.5 million people live around me. Residential contractors can survive and indeed make a nice living on as little as 30 customers a year. Even if you multiply that number by 10, as a contractor may service an average of 300 customers a year, there are still plenty of homeowners who will never hear of him, no matter how many people you tell to avoid him.

I knew of a residential heating and cooling company that had an unadvertised company motto of "One customer, one time." I asked about the meaning, and the reply was, "Customers are a royal pain. They think we overcharge every time and they are never satisfied. So we try to get as much money out of them as we can because we don't care if they call us back or not. Anyway, how often will they buy a new furnace in their lifetime?" This is clearly an attitude of a contractor who should get out of the business and one example of a company who doesn't worry about word-of-mouth.

Summary

Homeowners need to be aware that customers have committed fraud, misrepresentations, theft and sabotage against the contractor. Be sure to treat your contractor with respect and deal with him and his crew in a strictly professional manner. Customers can unknowingly set off red flags that warn the contractor to watch out, that he is about to be ripped off by the homeowner. Some red flags include:

1. Customer refuses to sign a Change Order form.

2. The husband and wife play good cop-bad cop.

3. Customers try to pit the employees against the contractor.

4. Customers make excuses for not keeping to the payment schedule.

5. The customer is constantly trying to get free work done that is not listed in the contract.

Your new understanding of the daily pressures dealt with by residential contractors will pay dividends to you in the selection process and provide the motivation for you to stick to the policy of *strictly business*. You will astound your contractor if you apply the principles of this book. Your rewards could be savings in the thousands of dollars, increased quality and services from your contractors and peace of mind.

Coming together is a beginning;
keeping together is progress;
working together is success.
—Henry Ford

6

GETTING THE MOST OUT OF YOUR CONTRACTOR

Respecting the Contractor's Time

Time is money to your contractor; you might think you purchased a new tub and a remodeled bathroom but the contractor knows that he really sold you his time. Time is the real commodity that the contractor sells. Respect your contractor's time.

Time is the primary cause of problems on the job. This can happen for a number of different reasons.

1. The contractor might have underestimated the time needed to complete the project to meet the professional standards of the trade.

2. The contractor's workers might make mistakes that cause additional lost time.

3. The homeowner may not have the rooms ready in a timely fashion, also causing lost time.

4. The homeowner may have asked for additional services, adding strain to the contractor's schedule because it makes sense to perform the work now.

5. Other homeowners may be putting pressure on your contractor to start or complete another project.

Time is the lifeblood in the body of work to be performed on your home. Time is the number one commodity in the residential service industries. Make sure, as the homeowner, you are not causing your contractor lost time. You can conserve and save the contractor's time by following these tips:

1. Be brief in your conversations, even if the contractor wants to talk at length.

2. Respect the stated work breaks and lunch periods for the crew.

3. Do not talk to the crew members while they are working.

4. Keep children and pets out of the way.

5. Make sure the driveway is clear for the crew every morning.

6. Make sure that the jobsite is in the same condition in which the crew left it the day before.

Helping to Keep Up Morale on the Job

The crew's morale on the job will affect the quality of work you receive and impact the value of the project for which you are paying. You do not control the morale of the crew or their interactions with the contractor. You may not control the morale of the crew but you *can* have an impact on it, be it positive or negative.

Following the guidelines in this book will help you have a

positive impact on the morale of the crew naturally. Complaining or inconsiderate behavior will most definitely bring down morale on the job.

To help keep morale high within the crews who are working on your project you should do the following:

1. Keep to the chain of command and never critique the crew-members directly. That is the job of the contractor and/or foreman. When you truly feel it, give out legitimate praise. A well-placed compliment at different stages of the project will go a long way. Many times individual workers on the crew do not feel appreciated and a kind word from you in recognition of their efforts can pay big dividends. When a particularly dangerous or tedious job is completed, you might offer a comment like, "You guys make it look so easy." Or, "I appreciate you being around to help with projects like this. I don't want my husband climbing ladders any more." Remember, deliver compliments only if you sincerely mean them.

> *People don't care how much you know until they know how much you care—about them.*
> *—Zig Ziglar*

2. Smile. Smile a lot. Be sure to be upbeat. Don't participate in the Monday morning blues. Remember this is business, *strictly business*, so if you want to receive the best possible outcome from the dollars you have invested, be upbeat around the crew. Even after you have filed a complaint, be upbeat. Lead with a positive attitude because you have everything to lose if you don't. If you are angry with the crew or their boss and you continually show it, you will be the

loser. Ask yourself who would work for a customer who is mad, or miserable to be around. Who would work for a person who leaves the crew with the feeling that no matter what they do, that customer will never be satisfied?

Sometimes the offer of a radio for listening will lift morale (though do not break your own rules). Serving cold drinks during hot working conditions or providing a warm place for breaks and lunch times during cold conditions can also do the trick. Be thoughtful but stay within the rules.

Morale can be high throughout the job if the crew believes the homeowner is reasonable; this can be achieved if you keep your end of the agreement. A homeowner who hassles the contractor with delayed payments will scare all the crewmembers as to what is going to happen next. When the job is nearing completion and you are satisfied with the progress, you can consider treating the crew to a pizza for lunch. It is not necessary to eat lunch with them, just have it delivered to your home at their designated lunchtime. Giving the crew a day or two notice so that they can anticipate it will buy you additional time for goodwill.

> *You get the best out of others when you*
> *give the best of yourself.*
> *—Harvey Firestone*

Strictly Business

When the crew and the contractor are in your home, do not discuss topics that can be controversial. Avoid topics such as religion, politics and drug use; also refrain from sharing personal information about yourself or other members of your household. Keep it professional. This can be difficult because you are in a very comfortable place, your home. Remember you have allowed strangers, or at least, not very well-known individuals, into your home. Keep your personal information personal.

Your policy is, "only on a need-to-know basis," and the members of your household should adhere to this policy at all times. You will share only the information that the contractor and the crew he has sent to your home need to know to complete the job. A *need-to-know policy* governing the flow of information protects your privacy and your investment. Another way to keep stress low for the crew is for your entire family not to argue, scream, yell and carry on a family dispute in front of the crew. Everyone feels uncomfortable when this happens. Tell your family to be on their best behavior.

Reducing Unnecessary Stress for the Crew

Never use Post-it® notes to identify flaws in workmanship unless asked to do so by the foreman or the contractor. Doing so without being asked will group you with customers who have demonstrated a complete breakdown in communications. Once again, you will send the stress level skyrocketing, and this can only lead to a diminishing return on your investment.

Another way to stress out a worker or the complete crew is to hover over them. Then be sure and tell them how they should do the work. Point out how they are wasting time and mention that you saw another company do it in a much better, faster and more professional way. This goes a long way to increasing the stress of the crew on the job.

Observing the work is acceptable. Just don't hover over the men. Asking good questions can also reduce the stress of the crew. "Is there anything I forgot that you need me to do today?

Did your boss tell you that he promised you would use drywall screws instead of nails? It sounds like you're using a staple gun to install the roof shingles and the contract calls for nails. Is that a staple gun I hear?"

When the crew is on a time schedule or when things are taking longer than expected to complete or when their boss is pushing them to move faster, you can reduce stress by taking care of the following:

1. Keep your pets under control.

2. Make sure the rooms are ready for them when needed and delivered in the required condition.

3. Ensure your children are not getting underfoot.

4. Keep the work zone clean and undisturbed after the crew has left for the day.

5. Clear lanes, stairways and driveways so the crew has easy access to your home.

If you are unclear on how successful you are at keeping unnecessary stress from the crew, ask yourself if you or something in your home is adding to the workload or if you are making the crew work harder than is really needed. For example, you may park your car close to your home so you have a short walk. However, this causes the workers to walk farther for their tools and supplies. You may also leave personal items lying around that impede the speed of the crew. If you are still unsure, ask the workers. They might not tell you in the most diplomatic way, but at least you will help reduce that stress for them. In doing so, you will increase your odds of getting the most out of the crew.

In the book, **Men Are from Mars, Women Are from Venus: A Practical Guide for Improving Communication and Getting What You Want in Your Relationships,** *author John Gray recommends starting your conversation with, "Honey, I know it's not your fault."*

Keeping to Your End of the Agreement

To the contractor you hired, the most important role you have is making timely payments. No excuses. If the contracting firm is holding to their end of the contract, then you must pay them per the payment schedule agreed to or you will send the stress level on the job site through the roof. Why? Because you will be acting like customers who have failed to pay the contractor in the past. Morale goes down, stress goes up, and everyone wonders if they are going to be paid. After all, they can never get back the *time* that they have spent on your project and they know it.

Summary

Respecting the contractor's time saves *you* time and allows the maximum amount of time for the professional execution of the services you have purchased. See yourself as a vital part of the checks and balances on the job and be sure of your role. Help keep morale high by keeping *your* morale high. Lead by example. It can only help and will never hurt your position.

Remember you are in the midst of a business transaction. If the crew is not working for you, they would be working for someone else. ***Strictly Business*** *is your motto.* If you get personal, you will be on a slippery slope. Make it personal and your emotions will lead you into a battle that you cannot win. Relieve stress when you see it building up, stick to your house rules and keep to your end of the agreement.

Remember that the contractor is in control of the execution of services and he can and will take short cuts if his frustration level is so high that he cannot wait to finish your project. Make sure you are reasonable, and that you are not the cause of unnecessary stress and you will be well on your way in getting the most out of your contractor and crew.

FOR EACH AND EVERY ACTION THERE IS AN EQUAL AND OPPOSITE REACTION

Action: *The homeowner informs the contractor and his crew that he has great neighbors, telling them, "Some of the neighbors literally watch everything that goes on in the neighborhood. So please don't mind if you see them checking you out."*

Reaction: *The contractor and his crew feel like someone could always be watching them.*

7

WHEN THE CONTRACTOR MOVES IN

Greeting the Crew

Y ou will have approximately 10 seconds to make a first impression on each crew member upon their arrival; the same goes for each crew member greeting you. Remember the *strictly business* attitude you want to convey. One of the best ways to greet the crew is to appear at your door with a drop cloth in your hand. Here is the ideal scenario.

You hear a knock on your door. You open the door to find the worker standing in his work boots and uniform or jeans. In your hand is a clean drop cloth approximately 5 feet wide by 15 feet long. You shake his hand and introduce yourself. If he is holding a drop cloth you say, "Oh, I can see we are going to get along fine. I was going to lay this drop cloth down to the work area, should we still use this one?"

If the worker doesn't have a drop cloth, after introductions say, "Here, let me lay this drop cloth down to the work area. I want us to keep things as clean as possible, is that OK with you?" In some residential service calls, a drop cloth could be a hazard. Asking the worker for approval starts a two-way conversation on how the work should proceed. It also establishes that you require due care and cleanliness of your property.

Be sure to meet each crew member and try to remember their names. Do not let a crew member work in your house without knowing his name. Look them all in the eye and shake their hands. Watch their body language. Who looks you in the eye, who doesn't? As soon as you get a chance, write down their names and a brief physical description to help you remember who they are. Share your notes with your spouse as well as other family members in your home. When possible, address them by their first names. If this seems a little over the top on detail, just remember this is *strictly business*. You don't know who on the crew, if any of them, that you can trust. Also, if you need to contact the owner or talk to the office over the telephone, names or physical descriptions will be helpful. If you have a lawsuit filed against you for any reason, your notes will become very important documents.

Next, if you are inclined to offer food and drinks to the crew, ask the contractor or foreman what time their first break will occur. Then inform them what food and drink is available and where it is located. If you are offering coffee or other hot drinks that require a cup or glass, put the cups and glasses out or you can expect the workers to be going through your cabinets looking for them.

At this first meet-and-greet, inform the crew of the following:

1. The location of the telephone

2. A list of contact telephone numbers in case of questions or emergencies

3. The location of the bathroom you wish them to use

4. The location of fire extinguishers

5. The location of the electrical box

6. The location of the gas and the main water shutoff valves.

Be sure to allow clear access to these areas in your home. If you plan to be home during the hours the crew is working you may not need to cover the list above until the item(s) are needed.

Setting the House Rules

The crew needs direction from the owner(s) on what is acceptable and unacceptable behavior in their home. If you fail to clearly define your rules, you reduce your chances of being completely satisfied by your contractor. You are also setting up a possible confrontation with the workers that can and should be avoided.

If you do not want the crew members smoking in your house, inform them right away. Placing an ashtray in the garage or out on the patio will send the message that it should be used. This rule might be stated as, "Guys, we don't allow smoking in our home and we have ashtrays out on the patio if anyone wants to smoke."

Many crews work with a radio on. Sometimes it is loud and the crew may listen to music or programming that is inappropriate for you and your family. Set the rules now: either no radio at all or only stations that you normally allow in your home. A good rule for volume is to have the radio only loud enough to be heard at a distance of five feet and never to be audible over any equipment such as power tools. Regardless of how long you expect the crew to be in your home, discussing radio use will help you establish control of the situation. If the project is expected to last for weeks or if something goes wrong and it ends up lasting longer, your nerves can be very frayed because you hear FM shock jocks, talk radio, country, hard rock, rap, classical, etc., for one more day. The day you plan to convince the crew to give up the radio or reduce the volume could lower morale, or it could be the day that their attitude toward you and the project takes a serious turn for the worse.

Be sure to address the rules concerning your pets. These may include allowing your pet to come and go as it pleases from indoors to outdoors or allowing the pet into certain parts of the house. If you don't allow people to pet your dog, tell the workers in advance, especially if your pet does not like strangers. Special attention may be required to control dust where fish tanks or bird cages are part of the household. If your pet likes to "escape" from the house or the yard, be sure to warn the crew. Ask them to be extra careful with opening and closing the doors or gates.

Make your policy on visitors clearly known to the crew. I have experienced cases where unwanted visits from in-laws, disgruntled contractors or adult children of the contractor or crew have come into the home when the owners are away from the house. Our company policy is to not let anyone into the home unless they have a key or the customer has told us to expect the visitor.

You need to discuss security issues and how you want them addressed; your wishes and desires *must* be followed. Make this clear to the contractor or foreman. If you give the foreman the key to your home, will he leave it in a lock box on-site or can he take it home? Find out who will have access to the key. The same policy applies for any codes for the alarm system. When possible, program your alarm with a temporary code just for the contractor and his crew. If at any time you find your home left in an insecure state, call the contractor or his office and inform them immediately. If the contractor has ladders or chemicals on-site, they could cause the risk of injury to your children or pets. Address your need for the crew to comply with your rules and have these items safely secured at all times.

Share with the crew the rules you have for the behavior of your children. For example: the children are not allowed in the work zone and if they do go into the area, you expect the crew to inform you immediately. Perhaps you have given one of the children the task of making sure the family pet stays out of the work zone. If so, let the crew know that you expect them to tell you if the pet is not kept under control.

Tell the crew that you are counting on their cooperation and that these rules are important to you and are your efforts to insure a successful project for everyone.

Establishing a Chain of Command

Two separate chains of command exist on every job. One is the contractor's and the other is yours. Find out who is the foreman and if he is the party responsible for the jobsite conditions and execution of the contract. If the foreman is not the person in charge, find out who is. Determine who is second in command on the jobsite if the foreman is not present. Also, tell the crew who is in charge of the project from your point of view. This should be either you or your spouse. If a house-sitter is present during the day while the crew is working, let them know what authority, if any, the house-sitter has. The same policy applies to your children. If you have a responsible teenager in your home that can take and give accurate messages, let the crew know where the teenager fits into your chain of command. Let the foreman know the chain of command concerning Change Orders. If you do not want your spouse approving additional work or additional labor, make it clear from the beginning.

Who Is In Charge?

The contractor is in charge and you cannot forget it. He is in charge of the jobsite, his crew, equipment, suppliers and supplies. You are in charge and you cannot forget it. You are in charge of your home, the jobsite after hours, your pets, your children, your spouse and most importantly, your checkbook. You both are in charge of adhering to the terms of the contract.

Establishing a Work Schedule

At the beginning of the project, find out the contractor's expectations for the timeline and work progression schedule. Asking their goal for the day is a perfect beginning for discussion of the schedule. Seek out their thoughts on how they see the job progressing. Listen to answers from either the foreman or the contractor *only* and do not place too much value in the opinion of any other crew member. Find out how many men will be assigned to your project and when you can plan to have the contracted work completed. Ask them if they will be at your home every single day until completion and if not, why? Find out if they plan to work weekends and what their daily hours are, including start time, quitting time and scheduled breaks. Tell them to inform you immediately if their schedule changes at all. This includes occasions when they may leave early with no intention of returning later in the day, delays due to weather or lack of supplies, or the need to work later than regularly scheduled hours including weekends.

FOR EACH AND EVERY ACTION THERE IS AN EQUAL AND OPPOSITE REACTION

Action: *A crew arrives to work on your project and the only member who speaks English is the foreman. A half-hour after the work begins, the foreman disappears from the jobsite.*

Reaction Homeowner: *After waiting one half-hour to see if the foreman returns, you call the contractor and inform him of the circumstances. You tell the contractor the situation is unacceptable because you're unable to communicate with the crew. You offer the following options: have the foreman return and stay on the job full time, if the foreman leaves all work stops, otherwise have a translator on-site at all times, or send out a different crew and reschedule your project if necessary. Tell the contractor good communication is very important to you. If he fails to choose from the options listed above, fire his company.*

Confirm when the next payment will be due based on the terms set forth in the contract. For example, "The contract calls for a second payment to be made when you have completed half the work or after a specific stage, such as when the landscaping is completed. What day do you expect that to be?"

If you have any concerns about the timeline, address them now with the foreman or call the contractor directly and get the issues addressed now, not later. You need to finalize the details at the initial meet-and-greet.

Once you have an established work schedule agreed to by everyone, be sure you meet your responsibilities in keeping on track with that schedule. Ensure that rooms are empty when needed and keep to the payment schedule to which you have agreed. Let the contractor know that you will keep to that schedule and that you require him to do likewise. Let him know that both of you agree to inform each other if something should happen that would keep either of you from adhering to the schedule.

Clarifying Lines of Communication

Establish a clear method of dealing with Change Orders. Will they all be in writing or are verbal orders binding? What does your contract say? What signatures are required? Will it affect the timeline? When will the price or cost of the Change Order be determined? Do you want the price given to you when the add-ons are completed or before any work begins? Do you expect the contractor to call you before starting any additional work not covered by the contract? If he can't reach you can he still proceed? Will you cover any costs that the contractor may incur if he cannot reach you and needs to stop working on the project? Clarify and inform the crew how you want Change Orders handled. Stick to the contract. If the contract does not address this issue, come to an agreement immediately. Following this advice can save you bundles of money in cost overruns, whether or not they are legitimate.

If your contractor cannot reach you during the day when he

has a question, do you prefer that he leave a written note (very good for your records) or can he call and leave a voice mail at home or at work? How will you communicate with the contractor or the foreman if they cannot be reached? Will the contractor take a fax from you (very good for your records) or will you leave the foreman a written note, voice mail, or e-mail? Come to an agreement and stick to it.

Summary

When the contractor moves in and you meet his crew, taking the time to get started on the most positive note possible is very important. Don't waste this opportunity.

Remember these steps:

1. Greet the crew.

2. Set your house rules.

3. Determine the chain of command.

4. Remember who's in charge and what each party's responsibilities are.

5. Establish a project schedule.

6. Determine and define the lines of communication.

Follow these steps and you will increase your odds of experiencing a positive, win-win business transaction.

What causes opponents to come of their own accord is the prospect of gain. What discourages opponents from coming is the prospect of harm.
—*Sun Tzu*

8

How To Fire A Contractor

Things can and will go wrong on projects that you hire out. When you have tried to resolve the issues in good faith and your efforts fail for any reason, it is time to fire the contractor. There are steps you need to take to protect both your rights and your property before you dismiss your contractor.

Getting the Contractor Out of Your Home

You need to follow these steps:

1. Determine the area(s) in which the contractor has breached the contract.

2. Gather evidence to prove your position and your case.

3. Double-check your paperwork—names, business license numbers, license plate numbers from company and crew vehicles, Change Orders, notes, messages, etc.

4. Take before and after pictures.

5. Make sure you have a copy of the contract in writing.

6. Identify the clauses the contractor failed to meet.

7. Locate all insurance papers, both his and yours. If you do not have this information, get it and organize it.

Depending on your situation, firing a contractor may or may not save you money. Are you sure of your position and what it will cost you in dollars and time to fire and rehire another contractor? What is it costing you to have the work done incorrectly? What can it cost you in additional repairs in the years to come? Consider seeking the opinion of your local building inspector. The building inspector is an independent source that can inform you if the work being performed on your home meets the standards of the trade as well as the local building code. He is an agent of the state. His opinion carries a lot of weight in the courts and at licensing hearings. Insist that the building inspector send you a letter describing the issues that you had him inspect, his evaluation of those issues, and the quality of workmanship that he has observed to date on your project. Ask him to make notations on his inspection form of any damaged property that exists while he is inspecting your home. You want to have the condition described on the inspection report without comment as to how or what happened. The building inspector may be uncomfortable making such notations, but assure him that you just want it acknowledged that the condition exists. This will provide you with a date, time and description of the condition by a government agent in writing.

The Reasonable Man Test

Now put your position to the "Reasonable Man" test. Look at the problem from the position of a disinterested third party. If you had an inspection done, what did the building inspector's report say? Is your position reasonable? How would a judge and jury view the position you are taking? Would you appear to be demanding too much? How would your story sound in a year from now? Does it appear reasonable? If the answer is no, start acting reasonably, so you can still fire the contractor if you need to.

A reasonable person will attempt to resolve issues before they get out of hand. However, if the contractor continues to fail to perform as promised, you must make a final attempt to resolve the issues. At your final attempt to resolve the issues, you will need a witness.

> *When forces angrily confront you but delay engagement, yet do not leave, it is imperative to watch them carefully.*
> *—Sun Tzu*

The witness you choose can be a relative or a friend. Be sure to select a person who can help you if the need arises. Ensure that they can be available as a witness at a hearing or trial. If a considerable amount of money is at stake, have your attorney and a witness present at the meeting. Just avoid introducing him as your attorney since this meeting is an attempt to resolve the issues at hand. If the attempts at the beginning of the meeting fail, you can always direct your attorney to take action at the end of the meeting.

Breach of Contract/Cease Operations

If this last attempt at resolution fails, you will be giving your contractor a "Breach of Contract, Cease Operations Until Further Notice" form (see Appendix L). You can post this notice outside of your home, on a door, or you can hand it to the contractor or his employee on the jobsite. Once this is done you still have some issues to deal with. The contractor has the right to collect his tools and equipment in a timely fashion. You must collect your keys if you entrusted them to the contractor. If you cannot get them back or the relationship is damaged to the point of no return, consider having your locks changed and charging back the cost to the contractor. You will also need to decide who will take control of the materials and supplies and you will need to determine a final bill.

> *When you come to the end of your rope,*
> *tie a knot and hang on.*
> *—Franklin D. Roosevelt*

Materials, Who Owns Them?

Does your contract show that you gave a deposit for materials or special custom-ordered items? You need to make your own list of the materials that have been installed or used on your project and compare it to the contractor's list. The contractor should provide receipts or statements from his suppliers that the items have been paid for in full. Without such proof of payment, the homeowner may be subject to liens being filed against their home by the suppliers. The materials can be a significant dollar amount, especially for custom-ordered appliances or items like granite countertops. The homeowner will have no idea if the contractor has placed stop-orders for custom materials and supplies in time to avoid suppliers charging him. Get written, verifiable proof that the contractor paid who he claims to have paid and canceled orders as he claims. Do not settle any monies due without receiving all the materials in good working, ready-to-install condition.

Be aware that if you choose to take ownership of the materials and supplies, you will assume the responsibility for them. It may be difficult to find another contractor who will use or install your materials and supplies. One reason is that the second contractor will not get to mark up the supplies and materials. Secondly, the materials and supplies may be different from that which the new contractor and crew are accustomed to working with, thus increasing the risk of additional labor for lost time due to a learning curve. This could lead to the homeowner paying more for the installation labor. Thirdly, the second contractor cannot be expected to warranty your supplies and materials. Think it through before deciding to take ownership of the materials and supplies. Do your homework.

Determining a Final Bill

The best chance for fairness is now. If you owe the contractor money, you are in the driver's seat. If the contractor is the cause of property damage or worse, if all the contractor's work has to be dismantled and redone by another contractor, he owes you money.

If the contractor wants more money from you for services performed at a professional level and you agree, then pay him for those services. At the very least, give him a credit for those services and deduct it from what he owes you.

If you plan to hire another contractor to redo the work or to complete the project, you must know the cost to settle. If you plan to live with the work supplied by the first contractor, you must pay him for his labor. You will be unable to make a case for not paying for services rendered. If you plan to hire another contractor to improve upon the first contractor's work, you will only need to charge back the additional costs you incur in bringing the first contractor's workmanship up to the standard of the trade. A contractor walking off the job without good cause is in breach of contract and is making a costly mistake. The contractor must be able to prove that the homeowner has breached the contract, otherwise the contractor may be held responsible for the additional costs needed to complete the job. Do not negotiate from this position. Getting a judgment and collecting funds are two very different phases of a court settlement. Remember, now is the chance for your best settlement. Avoiding a lawsuit is in the interest of both parties. Negotiate from a position of strength to settle this transaction now.

Summary

Don't be intimidated. Get the support you need to protect your interest. Document everything. Do your homework. If you need to use an attorney to negotiate a final bill, do so. If you are being unreasonable, your documents will work against you. Get everything in writing, including a final statement of mutual agreement to end your contractual relationship.

Once you have fired your contractor, sit down and evaluate who, what and when things started to go wrong. Learn from your mistakes, and from what you did correctly. Restart the search for a new contractor and stick to the *strictly business* attitude. Of course, do not tell the second contractor that you fired the first contractor. Reread Chapter 1: Choosing Your Contractors.

9

GAMES THAT HOMEOWNERS PLAY

The Stall

Homeowners have a contractor selection process that they use to determine who they will hire. Where they learned the process and how successful they are with it varies, but most homeowners fail with their system. The system starts with getting bids from different contractors. The homeowner uses the bid process to discover and get different opinions about how the work should or shouldn't be done, what materials should or shouldn't be used, and what price range the project might cost.

While the homeowner is gathering bids, they stall contractors with lies, misrepresentations and broken promises. They shop ideas and bids from individual contractors and attempt to play the contractors against each other. This stalling tactic is well known to good and reputable contractors. When the homeowner plays this game of stalling, the lies and broken promises can and will get in the way of a win-win business transaction.

Good Cop, Bad Cop

In this game, the homeowner uses his or her spouse as an excuse or threat. The game might start when the wife makes an excuse as to why the room is not ready, or why the check has not been signed or when any other contractual responsibility of the homeowner has not been met.

Common forms of the "good cop, bad cop" game occur on quality control issues where one spouse indicates that they are happy with the workmanship or progress of the job but they warn the contractor that, "You really have to speak to my husband because he is the real stickler for details." The husband usually does not make himself available and the wife continues to give the contractor the "thumbs up" as the work progresses. This game very quickly leads to misunderstandings and disputes. "Good cop, bad cop" does not allow mutual trust to develop on the jobsite between the homeowner and the contractor or his crew.

I Forgot

"I forgot" is the homeowner's excuse for not performing or executing their responsibilities for keeping the job moving. Examples include forgetting to deposit funds in the checking account, forgetting the checkbook at work, forgetting to leave the checkbook at home, forgetting to move your car, forgetting to remove your personal belongings out of the room, forgetting to unlock the door, etc. Your contractor has heard them all before.

If you *forget* to perform in a timely fashion and play this game on your contractor, you can expect your contractor to run out of patience. If the contractor becomes impatient with your forgetfulness, you can expect problems. Your forgetfulness is scaring him; he will worry that you are not paying attention to him and that you will cost him money in additional delays. This game might lead your contractor to take short cuts in advance to protect his budget from your forgetfulness.

You Should Have Known

When homeowners hire services out, they have a certain expectation of what type of service(s) they are hiring. The expectations in services can vary from very high to very low, depending on how the homeowner selected the contractor. Often when things start to go wrong on the job, the homeowner looks to protect both his pocketbook and his ego.

Here is one indication that the homeowner is protecting himself and his money. His contractor informs him of a problem and the homeowner begins his response with, "You should have known; you're the professional."

"You should have known" is a game played by homeowners in order to deny ownership of the problem. The homeowner wants the contractor to absorb the cost of an additional labor charge due to the condition of the jobsite. This is not the same as the contractor writing up a vague contract.

"You should have known" comes into play when the contractor discovers an unforeseeable condition that is the cause of an additional up-charge in labor due to an item not visibly apparent when the bid was given. An example of this might be the discovery of black mold that was not visible to the naked eye during a remodeling project.

"It's your fault" is another variation of "You should have known." Homeowners will try to play a game in which they expect the contractor to take responsibility for every item that causes the price to increase. This is the homeowner's version of the blame game. A homeowner who plays this game with the contractor and his crew is, in effect, saying, "You're the professional, protect me from myself."

Let's Pretend

In this game, the homeowner sends messages to the contractor and his crew that he (the homeowner) is OK and the contractor and his crew are also OK. Homeowners generally play this game when they feel that they must hide their concerns because they have difficulty expressing their true feelings. This type of homeowner seeks the crew's approval, thinking that the crew will perform better if they like the homeowner. Homeowners who play this game always hope that the contractor will fix the problem without being told to do so.

This game usually ends when the final payment is expected. Instead of getting a check, the contractor receives a 10-page punch list of complaints and concerns or finds a room with Post-it® notes pasted all over the place indicating problem areas.

> *It is a fact that you project what you are.*
> *—Norman Vincent Peale*

The Tease

This game usually starts at the estimate phase of contractor selection. The homeowner calls the service company out for a small to mid-size job. The homeowner indicates that he has many projects coming up and if the price is right, the contractor will be awarded the other jobs. In some cases, the homeowner convinces the contractor to discount his price in response to the promise of more work. Note that the contractor may or may not inform the homeowner of the discounting. Once the contractor realizes the homeowner will not deliver on the promise of more work, he will look for ways to recover his price reduction.

Summary

Do you recognize these games played with contractors? If you have hired many contractors over the years and have not developed a list of good service companies, perhaps you have been playing some of the games mentioned above.

Good contractors want to focus on their work, not the customer who wants to play games. A customer list of game players has very little value for the contracting company.

Homeowners have been pulling these tricks for years because they feel that game-playing gives them the upper hand. When homeowners win at these games, their contractors lose. The contractor can lose in the following ways: loss of production, loss of income, a drop in job-site morale, frustration and stress.

You can fool some of the contractors some of the time but you cannot fool all of the contractors all of the time. If you think you are the exception, the free marketplace will put the contractor out of business. Here is what it looks like. A homeowner reads this chapter and says, "I have certainly played some of these games, and I've done just fine." Upon questioning the homeowner, you will find that the last roofer or plumber that they used was excellent. The problem is that they just can't find him for their next job, or he isn't returning their calls for some reason.

It is in the homeowner's best interest to have an attitude

of *strictly business* so that there are no losers and all parties to the agreement end up in a winning position. Remember that the contractor is in control of the job site. Unless you watch *every* move, which is impossible, he and his crew can place you, your money, your home and your peace of mind at risk. Why play games? Choose to be professional. Be fair. You will become one of your contractor's best customers and he will treat you accordingly. Think win-win.

> *But this call to arms is not a call to do battle.*
> *It's a call to learning. How to feel, think, and act*
> *differently and more productively, more __humanly__ than our*
> *existing skills and understanding allow.*
> *—Michael E. Gerber*
> **The E Myth, Why Most Small Businesses Don't Work**
> **And What To Do About It**

10

TROUBLESHOOTING
HOW TO COMPLAIN TO YOUR CONTRACTOR

Think about your own work experience. How well do you or your fellow employees take criticism from your boss? How much understanding do you have of your current boss? How much experience do you have in the supervision of employees? Keep your mind on the big picture and figure out how to most effectively accomplish your goals. In a word, the best way to complain to your contractor is by using OPTIONS.

Lodging Your First Concern

Do you remember that first day when the contractor and his crew arrived? That day you established a clear chain of command. Now you will follow that chain of command when lodging your first concern. Ask the foreman or the leader of the crew if they have completed the task you are concerned about. If the answer is no, wait until they tell you that they are done with that phase or area of the project. Then re-inspect it to see if your concern was addressed without you even mentioning it to them. Give the workers plenty of space to do their jobs without interference.

If they answer that they have completed your area of concern, then ask them, "Since this area is completed, are you ready for me to look it over?" If they answer yes again, ask the foreman, "Is this a good time to address some concerns that I have?" Asking for permission gives the *impression* that the foreman has control. If the foreman answers that this is not a good time to discuss the issue, then ask for an appointment to address the concern and make sure that everyone keeps the appointment. You want the foreman to give you his full attention but if he has more pressing needs, such as keeping the rest of the crew working, you must respect his time. Remember this appointment is to address the first concern. You will not be inclined to be very cordial if you feel that the contractor or his foreman are putting you off or ignoring you.

Once you point out your concerns, your goal is to come to an understanding of how you want the finished product or service to appear. Avoid telling the foremen how to do his job. Ask the foreman when he thinks that this area will be addressed. Be sure to give the contractor sufficient time to fix the problem. Tell the foreman to let you know when he has corrected the issue.

If you are stalled on addressing and correcting the areas of concern, *do not make another payment to the company until your issues are completely resolved to your satisfaction.* Making a payment allows the contractor to continue ignoring you. If you make a payment, you will be ignoring your own concerns.

Feeling Ignored

If you are frustrated by the way your project is going, it is very likely that you are being ignored by the company that you are paying. This is a clear sign that the lines of communication have broken down. When your contractor is ignoring you and/or your project, try the following solution.

"Bob, this is Betty on Handy Road. Your crew has not worked on my home for two days now. I know I am not your most important customer, because if I were, your crew would be here finishing the work per our agreement. If you cannot keep up your end of the agreement, I need to know now so I can limit my expenses. When can I expect you to get back to working on my project or at least to let me know that our relationship is over?"

I once hired a landscaper to plant over 30 trees on my property. He came out, dug the holes in the ground and dropped the trees into them. The trees were left for over two weeks with the root balls still left in burlap. It rained and the trees were still soaking in three-foot holes filled with water. I called a friend who was in the landscaping business. He advised me to call my landscaper and tell him, "I know you have more important customers than me. However, my trees are completely soaked and have been for weeks. Even when the weather cleared up, you failed to contact me or come out to complete the transplanting. You can either replace all of the trees that you brought or extend the warranty for an additional year." My landscaper apologized for the delays, blamed the weather, assured me that the wet conditions would not damage the trees and chose to extend the full warranty for an additional year. Offering the options that I did allowed the landscaper to have control, yet protected my interests. In the end, the landscaper was right. All my trees survived without needing any replacement under warranty. Of course, I made sure the new agreement with the extended warranty existed in writing before I allowed the landscaper to finish transplanting the trees.

Leaking Roof

Suppose you hire a roofing contractor and the crew is caught in a rainstorm. Sometimes the roofer will install a blue plastic tarp over your roof to protect it from the coming rain. High winds come with the storm, however, and the tarp blows loose, causing water to leak into one of your rooms.

Your roofer apologizes and informs you that they did their best but sometimes things like this just go wrong. He offers to fix the drywall damage and paint the ceiling in the room in which the water damage occurred. You offer to have your painter do the work but he says that he wants to take care of it himself, or that he knows of a good painter he can call. You are relieved that he will be taking responsibility and that the water damage will not cost you any money. *Do not fall for this offer by your roofer.*

The water-damaged area needs to dry out. Painting too soon will trap the water in the ceiling drywall and the paint will peel again within 18 months. Do not settle with your roofer. Do not pay him for the new roof he installed, at least until your home is made whole again. The proper way for your roofer to respond is to turn your water damage claim over to his commercial liability insurance company and pay the deductible. Most roofers will be reluctant to do so, since they do not want to pay their deductible or have your claim go against their record. Do not let your roofer turn his crew into drywall installers and painters, either. If you do let the roofers fix the damaged area they will not, and could not, offer you any warranty on this work. Also, if the roofers fix the damaged area, your homeowner's insurance will not cover any future claims you may make on your ceiling. If the roofers cause further damage to your property while making the repairs to the ceiling, their insurance will not cover them since they are performing outside the area of their trade, which is roofing. If you use the painter supplied by the roofing company, the painter will be working for the roofing company—not you.

If you have followed the advice of this manual, you should have a copy of the roofer's insurance papers. Send your original copy of the roofing contract and the proof of insurance to his insurance company and their adjustor should contact you. Do not delay in making your claim; if you wait, you may lose some, if not all, of your rights to file a claim. Try to enlist the cooperation of your roofer and have him file the claim with his insurance carrier himself.

If your roofer and his insurance company will not cooperate with you, file a claim with your homeowner's insurance carrier. Withhold the amount of your deductible from the final payment to the roofer. Provide your insurance company with copies of the roofing contract and the roofer's proof of commercial liability insurance. Your insurance company may choose to pursue a settlement on your behalf with the roofer's insurance company. The insurance company that ends up covering your loss will allow you to hire a professional painter to repair the damage. The painting company that performs the repairs will provide you with a copy of their insurance papers and should warranty the work to protect you from future paint failure on your ceiling. The painter you select will also be working for you and not the insurance company.

Poor Surface Preparations

Regardless of the trade, when dealing with poor surface preparations, approach the contractor and say, "I understand the crew considers this area to be ready for the next step. My concern is that the (enter your concern here). When do you expect it to be corrected?" If the contractor tells you that the surface preparations you have received are as good as it is going to get, you have a problem.

Look to your contract for a description of the surface preparations. If the contract states, "Work to be performed to the standard of the trade," find out what those standards are (See Appendices). Acquire copies of the standard in question, find the areas that address your issues and give a copy to your contractor. Hold to your position if indeed the standards support your claim that the surface prep falls below those standards. If the contractor still disagrees or refuses to correct the areas of concern, make the following options clear to him:

1. You can have the building inspector out to determine who is right, the contractor or you.

2. The contractor can proceed as he wishes and if the final appearance is unacceptable and below standards, he agrees to rework the area in question until it is professionally done. You will suspend all payments until the work passes inspection.

3. He can stop working on the project and you will hire another company to perform the work to the standard of the trade.

Failure To Perform As Promised

You determine that the services purchased at the time of the sale are not being delivered as promised. Meet with your contractor and say, "Before we invest any more time and money, we need to clarify exactly what I have purchased and what you sold me concerning the following..."

Rewrite the contract, or sign a Change Order form for clarity if needed. Have a meeting of the minds and proceed with a clean slate so everyone will end up with a win-win transaction.

Questionable Material Choice

Let us suppose that you notice that some of the materials being used on your project look suspect, damaged, or of a lower grade or carry a different model number than that which you ordered. Do not allow your contractor to install discontinued or closeout products without receiving a guarantee and confirming that the manufacturer will honor the warranty. Your contractor may have purchased products at a discount and may be planning to install them in your home. The discount may have been given because parts are no longer available to service these products in the future.

If in doubt, call the suppliers or check on the Internet for the specific model or product numbers and inquire about purchasing them. Ask the manufacturer about the availability and serviceability of the products. If you decide that you do not want the products that the contractor purchased to be installed, find out if the contractor can get a refund, what the cost was for the products, and how much more it will cost you to upgrade the products. Come to an agreement with the contractor and get it in writing.

They Did It Anyway

Suppose you instruct the contractor as to how you want something to be done or installed. It is clear that you have reached an understanding. The contractor or his crews have a miscommunication and the service is not performed as directed. What can you do?

Get bids from other legitimate contractors to undo the contractor's mistake and to have the work re-done correctly. First, try to get the contractor to honor the agreement. Then, present the bid(s) to the contractor if they are unwilling to correct their error.

I know of a woman who had an extensive remodeling project consisting of a two-story addition to her home. She had ordered stain-quality wood trim, including a patio door wall unit, replacement windows and crown moldings. She came home one day to find that the painters had painted all the woodwork instead of staining and varnishing. The contractor then refused to replace or strip and stain the woodwork. Instead, he offered to paint her living room for "free." She settled on having the living room painted. To this day, she is still dissatisfied with her choice to settle and wished she had known that she had the right to insist that the contractor replace the woodwork.

Taking a settlement offer is OK as long as you won't regret not getting the job done the way you want. Ask yourself how you will feel about the project in 12 or 24 months. Always go for peace of mind. If the contractor will not fix it, hire a second contractor to fix the problem and deduct it from the first contractor's final bill. Of course, be sure to first give the offending contractor the option to fix it properly.

They Violated Your House Rules

If the violation is minor, remind the foreman of the house rules and ask him to make sure that the crew adheres to them. If the offense is major, contact the contractor/owner of the company and insist that the offending employee be removed from your project. If the contractor informs you that the employee is critical to completing your project, inform him that you have a serious problem and it needs to be addressed immediately. Give the contractor options such as: stop working on your project until he can find another person to replace the offender, deduct that part of the contract from the bill or find another contractor to finish that phase of the project. Your home is your castle and you are the king or queen. Stand up for and enforce your house rules or the crew may walk all over you and your home.

> *Speak softly and carry a big stick; you will go far.*
> *—Theodore Roosevelt*

Feeling Intimidated

If the contractor or his crew is trying to intimidate you in any way, consider doing the following, depending on the circumstances: get a witness, stay calm, control your emotions, call the police, call the building inspector and/or file a police report. Record the dates, times, specific facts about the intimidating behavior, names of the offenders and your feelings and reaction to them.

A Contractor's Market

A contractor's market occurs when the demand for residential contractors is high due to strong remodeling and commercial markets. A soft market for contractors exists if new construction is down in both the residential and commercial construction markets at the same time. Why is this significant? In a soft market, the contractors who normally work on new construction both in the commercial and residential areas will seek work in the residential remodeling and maintenance markets. Be *very* cautious about hiring a company whose main business focus is commercial, industrial or new residential. These companies and their crews are not trained to be in homeowner-occupied homes and they are only reluctantly bidding on and performing work for you as a last resort. If they should secure a large job in the area of their focus, they will drop or delay your project without a second thought.

When the demand for residential contractors is high in your area and there is a shortage of good contractors, don't complain, your local economy is strong. Instead consider using one of the following options:

1. Find a good contractor and be willing to wait for him. Sign an agreement with him along with a completion date for the work.

2. Ask the contractor you want to hire if he has a slow season, such as winter or around the holidays. If you are willing to wait, sign up in advance for that period.

3. Hire the best contractor you can find, *but have enough money to pay for the project twice*. This strategy will allow you the option to fire the contractor if he fails to perform as promised.

Having enough funds available will reduce your stress and help you keep your emotions under control. These options will help protect your investment so that you will know you do not have to settle for anything less than professional work.

4. Wait until there is a change in the market conditions in your area. If the demand for contractors is very high and you are not able to hire a qualified contractor, just wait. You will not regret waiting for a good contractor, but you could regret hiring the wrong contractor forever.

> *Getting something done is an accomplishment;*
> *Getting something done right is an achievement.*
> *—Unknown*

Dealing with Insurance Companies

If you experience an insured loss on your home and need contractor services, keep the following points in mind:

1. An insurance company cannot tell you whom to hire and whom to allow into your home to perform repairs.

2. If you provide the insurance company with three bids they may average them out and offer you less than they should.

3. Insurance companies have a knowledge base of the current market rates for each trade in your area.

4. The insurance company will require you to sign papers acknowledging that you hold them harmless for any workmanship issues.

5. Any contractor sent to you via the insurance company may be more loyal to the insurance company than to you.

Having a good contractor on your side when dealing with an insured loss is invaluable. Being on the preferred customer list of a reputable contractor long before a natural disaster hits your area is priceless when it comes to getting in line for necessary repairs.

When angry, count ten before you speak;
if very angry, one hundred.
—Thomas Jefferson

11

STORIES FROM THE
FRONT LINES

The battle continues daily in our residential neighborhoods. There are casualties and victims. The following stories are true, some are known nationally, others are stories I experienced or learned from other contractors and homeowners. The names of the players have been omitted. These stories are included so that you might benefit from the lessons others have learned the hard way.

Kidnapped

In Utah, a teenage girl is kidnapped from her bedroom one night. Months later, she is found with her kidnapper walking the streets of her hometown and she denies her identity to the police. The kidnapper was a person her mother hired to work on their roof.

Before the police found the girl, their investigation showed the parents had previously hired a subcontractor who had a 30-year criminal record and admitted to stealing from them. The parents have a history of suspect hiring practices. Their daughter paid a high price for their poor judgment.

Conspiracy

A national television talk show personality discovered his painter plotting to kidnap his 16-month-old baby and nanny. The painter pleaded down the charges and was sentenced to 10 years in prison. He had a criminal past.

Assault

In Pennsylvania, a retired handyman was arrested for kidnapping and assault; he was charged for holding five women against their will in his basement. This is another example of the lesson that you never know who you are hiring, even for the smallest of jobs.

Firestarter

A homeowner hires two "painters;" they use six coats of paint to paint a foyer and stairway yellow. At the end of the job, they try to collect for the additional coats applied. The homeowner doesn't agree to pay the additional charges and informs the painters that he isn't going to pay them because they are not licensed and they should have used a primer.

The painters leave and return 15 minutes later. They knock on the door; the homeowner is shocked to see one painter sprinkling gasoline along the foundation of his home. The other painter asks the homeowner, "Are you sure you don't want to pay us?" The homeowner writes a check and the painters warn him if the check is not good, they will be back with matches.

A Picture Is Worth How Much?

My crew was painting for our customer, an elderly widow. She approached us and complained that the roofers working on her home had just informed her that they discovered additional wood rot and would need an extra $850 over the bid price to complete the job. I asked if she had an instant camera. She gave the camera to the roofer and asked him to take a picture of the wood rot. The roofer complied and brought the picture and camera back to the woman with an adjusted price, reducing the additional labor $400.

1...2...3...Testing

After repairing a bedroom ceiling, upon inspection of our plaster work, we could tell the plaster didn't dry right. We got permission from the homeowner to test a recent roof repair using a garden hose working off of a 28-foot ladder. After simulating a driving rain from all directions, we climbed into the attic crawl space to see if the leak was really fixed. It was raining in her attic. The homeowner was furious; her roofer had repaired the area three times assuring her the leak was fixed. In this case, the fourth time was the charm. A new roofer also helped get better results.

The Rest of the Story

Buried inside a local paper, a headline reads, "Guns Stolen From Home;" the accompanying article describes the crime of antique guns being taken from a home while the owner was out of town. The story below is what they didn't report. The homeowner contacted me and asked if I would complete the work of another painting contractor. This is always a red flag to a contractor. So naturally, I asked what happened to the other contractor. The homeowner hired an uncle and nephew team who worked together to repaint a few rooms to prepare the house for sale. Her ailing husband was sleeping in the living room because of all of the medical equipment and the size of the bed he needed. She also said she was moving out of the city because she needed help in caring for her elderly husband, so her sister opened up her home to them and would help with the husband's care. The "painters" she hired noticed two antique rifles in the basement and asked the woman if she would sell the guns to them. She said no, her husband was going to give them to their grandson.

Two days later, on Saturday, the husband was transferred via ambulance to his sister-in-law's home. On returning home on Sunday, the homeowner discovered the break-in and the missing guns. She called the police, and the investigation showed the nephew "painter" had a criminal record. The window was broken from the inside and the thief neglected to break the exterior storm window, so the thief failed to hide the fact they entered with a key. On Monday morning the police greeted the painters in her kitchen. They grabbed the painters by the scruff of their necks and sent them sprawling onto the backyard lawn. The police warned them not to work in their city anymore and then the officer pointed a finger at the homeowner and said, "Now go hire a licensed contractor."

The woman explained that she found the uncle and nephew team from their ad and it was right next to my advertisement in her local paper, the same newspaper that reported the crime.

Hard To Swallow

A woman hired a local carpet cleaning company to clean her first floor carpets. The woman went about her morning routine of feeding her children and getting them ready for school. Upon completing the work, one worker asked for payment and another employee asked to use the bathroom. The homeowner was surprised that the worker chose to use the bathroom located upstairs. An hour after the carpet cleaning crew left her home, the woman noticed that the diamond ring she left on the counter in the upstairs bathroom was missing.

She called the police, who ran a background check on the employees and discovered one of them had a criminal history. They questioned the employees at the carpet cleaning business and the thief admitted to taking the ring. He told the police that he swallowed the jewelry. The police had the thief recover the ring in due time. Last reported, the woman wasn't sure she wanted to wear the ring anymore, knowing where it had been.

Burial Scene

A young couple having their dream house built had the following experience. The husband appeared on the construction site unannounced and found the construction workers gathered out in the backyard. To his surprise, they were burying a 10-foot-diameter tire. A piece of equipment had gotten a flat tire and burying it was cheaper than hauling it to a landfill. The husband had to argue with the men to convince them to stop.

Delays Cost You Money

Executing their dream of retiring down south became a reality and a couple hired a home builder referred to them by good friends. The friends had used the builder to build their own home and were very satisfied. Problems began, and before the couple filed criminal charges against the builder, they discovered that this builder had other legal problems chasing him from another state. Before this referred contractor moved on to another victim, he installed the drywall in the home before the air conditioner was installed. The new home sat through delay after delay until mold formed on the installed drywall. The homeowner had to replace all of the drywall and spent tens of thousands of dollars making corrections to the home before moving in.

Step By Step

A customer approached me informing me her Civil War silver stein was missing and was valued between $900 and $9,000. She asked if I ever had a problem with any of my men dealing with theft. I informed her I never even so much had an accusation made against my men. She said. "Good, please don't say anything to them, maybe the stein would show up." I explained that if she was right about the theft there were five suspects. She was surprised that I said five. I explained to her that it wasn't just my three-man crew but also myself and her housekeeper. She said, "Oh no, my housekeeper has been working for me for over eight years." I explained that an ideal time to steal something was when four strangers were in the house.

I was concerned about the accusation, especially since the homeowner owed me $9,000. I wasn't sure if this customer was setting me up for an excuse not to pay the final payment. I had never worked for this woman before and our business relationship was in its first transaction stage.

The woman told me she would be contacting her appraiser to have a value placed on the stein. A week passed and we completed the work. The customer was satisfied and it was time to collect the final payment. When I asked for the payment, the homeowner responded that her appraiser didn't get back in touch with her and wanted to know what we were going to do about the missing silver stein. At this point, I was extremely anxious; I believed my crew, who told me that they remembered the customer showing us the stein but that it was later removed from the room.

At this juncture, even though I felt uncomfortable, I asked the homeowner if she would allow me to search her home for the stein. She agreed to the search. Once she agreed to such a request I started to believe her more; most people would not let a contractor go through the cabinets and drawers throughout their home. I checked out the kitchen, no luck, the dining room, no luck. I wanted to leave with a check for the balance due, not a postponement of payment waiting for an appraiser's opinion on the value of the missing stein. In the living room hutch, I found the stein tucked behind a stack of towels. At this point I was relieved, but wondering if I just sidestepped a scam attempt by this customer. Her reaction was one of relief and she stated, "I must have put it there for safe-keeping." I was paid in full for the work performed. A week later, the same customer gave me a deposit to have her exterior painted. It wasn't until she hired us for the exterior that I knew with certainty that this customer was dealing honestly with me all along. Her strictly professional/business approach to the issue of the missing stein and my professional response to her concerns laid the foundation for a great business relationship. We both kept our emotions under control even while dealing with the stress of a possible theft or the potentiality of non-payment.

Like A Good Neighbor

Each week, a homeowner rewarded his two-man landscaping crew with a cold six pack of beer. He left the beer near the garage door as a thank you when his lawn was done. The crew mowed his lawn every week on the same day before noon. Would you like your home to be the next lawn cut by these landscapers?

One for the...Ladder

A homeowner offered a masonry contractor some scotch; he accepted and they converse. The contractor pressures the homeowner every day for another drink. The masonry contractor was repairing a two-and-a-half story chimney. I guess the drink helped steady his nerves. The customer complained that the contractor spent more time drinking his scotch than working on the chimney.

Blindsided

A very busy working couple allowed carpet installers access to their home while both were at work. Six months later, they get a certified letter explaining they are being sued for $25,000 by one of the carpet layers. Calling the carpet store, they discovered the person filing the lawsuit worked for the subcontractor the carpet store uses to install carpeting. The carpet store claimed they are not part of the lawsuit since it is not an employee of theirs. They further inform the homeowners that they were not aware of any injuries suffered by "their" carpet installers. The lawsuit claimed the worker fell down the steps, injuring his back.

Nothing Like a Strong Foundation

Homeowners hired a contractor to construct a foundation for their modular home. Modular homes are built off-site and delivered in two halves to the homeowner's property. They are built with 2x6s instead of 2x4s because of the higher stress tolerances needed to transport and the "dropping" of the two halves onto the foundation.

When the home was delivered, the installation crew discovered that the contractor built the foundation incorrectly. The foundation measurements were off; the contractor who built the foundation compensated by adding cement blocks next to the walls to widen the foundation. The contractor filed suit once the homeowner refused to pay him. The homeowner's attorney discovered the contractor was unlicensed and his client didn't have to pay the contractor. The homeowner's home warranty on the modular home was in jeopardy because of the faulty foundation. The homeowner should never have allowed the home to be installed on the foundation that did not meet the manufacturer's specifications. I'm sure they felt pressure from all fronts—time, expense, delays and a need to move in. Perhaps they weren't even on-site when the house was delivered.

Price LESS

A good customer gives a top-quality builder a referral to a friend who is a doctor. The builder assumes the referral is a worthwhile investment of his time. He travels across town to the doctor's home and is awarded the contract.

Throughout the job, the busy doctor and his wife argue over their wants, desires and needs. The contractor works well with them and helps them along.

The doctor leaves town on business. The wife continues with changes she desires. The contractor has the wife sign the Change Orders.

The doctor comes home and refuses to honor the signed Change Orders. His reasons include that he doesn't like the changes his wife made and he didn't authorize them.

The builder files a lawsuit and discovers the doctor's wife is not listed on the deed to the property. Therefore she has no authority to approve changes. The case drags on for years. When the case is finally resolved by the court system, the builder ends up getting 10 cents on the dollar after all expenses are paid to go to trial.

Can You HEAR Me Now?

A contractor sues an Academy Award winning actor for 1.5 million dollars. The reason given by the contractor is that the actor and his wife refuse to pay for the Change Orders. Communicate, communicate, communicate.

Go To the Mattress

The homeowner warns the contractor that her cats can be spiteful when their space is invaded. She advises the crew to remove the drop cloths from the cats' favorite areas each night to reduce the odds of the cats using the drop cloths as a litter box.

The woman explains that when the carpenters were in their bedroom the previous week, the cats urinated on their new mattress. She said they tried everything to clean the mattress but nothing could remove the smell. Two days later her husband comes home early from work and offers the crew a "like-new mattress" free to any of the crew members who want to haul it from his garage. He had no idea that the crew was aware of the history of the mattress. What was the husband thinking when he made the offer? Perhaps he believed the mattress was fine because he couldn't smell the urine. Perhaps he thought if one of the crewmembers hauled the mattress away he wouldn't have to haul it to the curb. Who knows, who cares what he was thinking? He impacted each worker differently as individuals. Nobody thought he was a nice guy because of his generosity.

Summary

This chapter recounts stories where the contractor and the homeowner went to battle. Some were mere skirmishes, others were life threatening. There are millions of these stories in the marketplace. When the homeowner and contractor make peace, they both create an opportunity to reach win-win in their business transaction.

When full-scale war breaks out, the terms of surrender are negotiated in a court of law. In court, a jury of the homeowner's peers and/or the judge will try to apply the "reasonable man test." The contractor will never be in front of a jury of his peers. It doesn't exist; one such jury would never be allowed to sit in judgment of a lawsuit. If you end up in court, the judge, jury and every reasonable person on the planet will know the following: you chose to invite and do business in your home with the contractor, both of you failed to communicate professionally, both of you made mistakes. You will be asking the judge and jury to assign blame. Even if you win a judgment, you still chose the wrong contractor. Going to court is like yelling at the top of your lungs, "I give up, what a mess I am in!" Everyone loses when you end up in court. What percentage of blame will be assigned to you?

Choose your contractors well. Apply the principles of this book. Develop a good working relationship with your contractors and enjoy your home, you deserve to.

> *Success is peace of mind*
> *in knowing you did your best.*
> *—John Wooden*

GUIDE TO APPENDICES

The appendices provided on the following pages can lead you to great sources and aid you in many ways. Many listed sources will point you to the "standard of the trade" for the profession you need to hire. One such source is the Painting and Decorating Contractors of America (PDCA). This organization has established 15 Standards for the painting and decorating trade. A helpful standard for both the homeowner and the painting contractor is the definition of a properly painted surface. PDCA Standard P1-04 2.2 reads:

> The Painting and Decorating Contractor will produce a "Properly painted surface." A "Properly painted surface" is defined as uniform in appearance, color, texture, hiding and sheen. It is also free of foreign material, lumps, skins, runs, sags, holidays, misses, or insufficient coverage. It is also a surface free of drips, spatters, and spills or overspray caused by the Painting and Decorating Contractor's workforce. In order to determine whether a surface has been "properly painted" it shall be examined without magnification at a distance of thirty-nine (39) inches or one (1) meter, or more, under finished lighting conditions and from a normal viewing position."

This description of a properly painted surface clearly spells out the contractor's responsibility, and how and under what conditions his work will be judged.

Appendix A

Painting & Decorating Resources

Painting & Decorating Contractors of America
www.pdca.com

Paint Quality Institute
www.pqi.net

Appendix B

Roofing Resources

National Roofing Contractors Association: www.nrca.net

American Society for Testing and Materials (ASTM)
www.astm.org

Midwest Roofing Contractors Association: www.mrca.org

The Western States Roofing Contractors Association
www.wsrca.com

CRCA Chicago Roofing Contractors Association
www.crca.org

North/East Roofing Contractors Association
www.nerca.org

The Iowa Roofing Contractors Association
www.iowaroofingcontractors.com

The Virginia Association of Roofing Contractors, Inc. (VARC)
www.varc.com

Slate Roofing Contractors Association of North America
www.slateroofers.org

Ohio Roofing Contractors Association
www.ohioroofing.com

Connecticut Roofing Contractors Association (CRCA)
www.crcainc.org

Independent Roofing Contractors of California, Inc.
www.ircc.org

New Mexico Roofing Contractors Association
www.nmrca.com

International Code Council
www.iccsafe.org

Appendix C

Drywall & Plaster Resources

Gypsum Association
www.gypsum.org

United States Gypsum Company
www.usg.com

National Gypsum Company
www.nationalgypsum.com/products

International Code Council
www.iccsafe.org

Appendix D

Plumbing, Heating, Cooling Resources

Plumbing Web
www.plumbingweb.com

Plumbing, Heating, Cooling Contractors Association
www.phccweb.org

Plumbing Links
www.plumbinglinks.com

Appendix E

Carpet Cleaning & Installation Resources

Carpet and Rug Institute
www.carpet-rug.com

Independent Carpet Inspectors & Experts
www.carpetinspector.com

Institute of Inspection, Cleaning Restoration Certification
www.iicrc.org

Appendix F

Home Appliances Resources

Association of Home Appliance Manufacturers
www.aham.org/consumer

Appendix G

Homeowner Resources: State Government Web Addresses for Licensing Information, Contractor Search Engines, & Consumer Complaint Forms

Go to these websites to research your rights and information about your contractor and his business and/or corporation. Some states do not require contractors to be licensed. The states that do not have specific trade licensure laws to protect you will have consumer protection laws that could provide you with certain remedies. Look for consumer information with the attorney general's office. Contractors may be required to have a local license if your state does not have license requirements at the state level.

Alabama
www.genconbd.state.al.us

Alaska
www.dced.state.ak.us/occ/pcon.htm

Arizona
www.azroc.gov

Arkansas
www.state.ar.us/clb

California
www.cslb.ca.gov/consumers/default.asp

Colorado
www.colorado.gov/colorado-doing-business/get-license-prmits.html

Connecticut
www.ct.gov/dcp

Delaware
http://onestop.delaware.gov/osbrlpublic/Home.jsp

Florida
www.myflorida.com

Georgia
www.georgia.gov

Hawaii
www.hawaii.gov/dcca/areas/pvl/boards/contractor/e_services

Idaho
www2.state.id.us/ag/consumer

Illinois
business.illinois.gov/licenses.cfm

Indiana
www.state.in.us

Iowa
www.iowaworkforce.org/labor

Kansas
www.kansas.gov/government

Kentucky
ag.ky.gov/consumer

Louisiana
www.lslbc.louisiana.gov

Maine
www.maine.gov/portal/business/licensing.html

Maryland
www.dllr.state.md.us/license/home_imprv/mhiclaw.htm

Massachusetts
www.mass.gov/bbrs/hic.htm

Michigan
www.cis.state.mi.us/bcs_free/default.asp

Minnesota
www.cis.state.mi.us/bcs_free/default.asp

Mississippi
www.msboc.us

Missouri
www.ago.mo.gov/Consumer-Protection.htm

Montana
http://mt.gov/services/business.asp

Nebraska
www.dol.state.ne.us/nwd/center.cfm

Nevada
www.nvcontractorsboard.com/default.htm

New Hampshire
doj.nh.gov/consumer/index.html

New Jersey
www.state.nj.us/nj/consumer/consumer/index.html

New Mexico
www.contractorsnm.com/search

New York
www.state.ny.us

North Carolina
www.ncdoj.com/consumerprotection/cp_about.jsp

North Dakota
www.ag.state.nd.us/CPAT/CPAT.htm

Ohio
www.com.state.oh.us/elicense.aspX

Oklahoma
www.oag.state.ok.us/oagweb.nsf

Oregon
www.oregon.gov/CCB/index.shtml

Pennsylvania
www.licensepa.state.pa.us

Rhode Island
www.crb.ri.gov/search.php

South Carolina
www.llr.state.sc.us

South Dakota
www.state.sd.us

Tennessee
www.tennessee.gov/commerce/boards

Texas
www.trcc.state.tx.us

Utah
https://secure.utah.gov/llv/llv

Vermont
www.vermont.gov

Virginia
www.dpor.virginia.gov

Washington
www.lni.wa.gov

West Virginia
www.labor.state.wv.us

Wisconsin
www.wisconsin.gov/state/core/business.html

Wyoming
attorneygeneral.state.wy.us

Appendix H

Miscellaneous Resources

The Associated General Contractors of America
American Subcontractors Association, Inc.
Associated Specialty Contractors

www.constructionguidelines.org

International Code Council

www.iccsafe.org

American Society for Testing and Materials (ASTM)

www.astm.org

Appendix I

Checklist for Contractor Selection

Research the legal requirements for state licensing or local certification requirements.

1. Gather business names.

2. Review advertisements and identify licensed/certified contractors.

3. Verify licensing or certification requirements have been met. Search online or call local governing body.

4. Write down name of licensee, full address and year licensed acquired.

5. Call companies on your list that meet local and state legal requirements and ask them to fax you proof of insurance for commercial liability insurance and workers compensation insurance.

6. Call their insurance carrier and verify insurance policy is still in effect.

7. Write down a clear description of your project.

Appendix J

Checklist for the Interview

1. Observe contractor upon greeting him. Take note of mannerisms. Is there eye contact? Does he conduct himself in a professional manner?

2. Describe the project. Take notice if the contractor listened to your description without interrupting you.

3. Listen and observe how the contractor responds to your description of the project.

4. Take notice if the contractor describes how he does business. Is the contractor vague?

5. Take notice if the contractor answers your questions or ignores them.

6. Take notice if the contractor is a good listener.

7. Take notice if the contractor writes detailed or vague job descriptions on his proposal.

8. Ask the integrity check questions.

   a) Who owns the company?

   b) Where is the company located?

   c) How long has he been in business?

   d) Did the contractor bring up the issue of subcontracting? Ask the contractor if he uses subcontractors. Get him to put the answer in writing.

9. Price check. Ask the contractor "What is your cash price?" Does he drop his price? If he does, did he drop labor? Do you want to do business with someone who did not bid the lowest price to you as a normal business practice?

10. Is this your guy? Are all promises in writing along with a detailed description of scope of work?

   a) No subcontractors

   b) Warranties

   c) Guarantees

   d) Brand and quality of materials

   e) Name of insurance carriers

   f) Notice of option to cancel

   g) Special instructions in writing

   h) Whose standard of the trades?

11. Decide to hire or not, schedule another appointment or postpone the project until you can afford to hire the right contractor.

12. Repeat this process until you find a contractor who has proven to you that he practices good business procedures.

13. Remember that if you can't afford to hire an honest contractor, you put yourself, your family, your home, your money and your peace of mind at risk in hiring a dishonest one.

Appendix K

Checklist for When the Project Begins

1. Drop cloth in hand, greet the contractor at the door.

2. Establish chain of command, both yours and the contractor's.

3. Inform contractors and his employees of your house rules.

4. Direct contractor to the location of: telephone, list of telephone numbers where you can be reached, bathroom you wish them to use, fire extinguishers, electrical box, gas and water main shutoff valves.

5. Keep driveway clear for easy access by contractor.

6. Have room(s) in ready-to-work conditions.

7. Secure all breakables and valuables in a secure space.

8. Establish a work schedule.

9. Establish a clear method of dealing with Change Orders, written or verbal. Who has authorization power for Change Orders?

Appendix L

Notice of Breach of Contract

Change Order

Forms can be downloaded at

www.how-to-hire.com

INDEX

S

T

V

W

ABOUT THE
AUTHOR

As a Residential Maintenance and Alteration Contractor for 28 years in Michigan, Carmen has been working in a living laboratory of residential homes. A customer base that transcends all social and economic experiences in the residential marketplace provided the environment where Carmen learned and developed the insight into the homeowner/contractor relationship. Carmen's problem-solving abilities are a requirement for success in the painting and decorating trades and he honed these skills in homes just like yours. Real-life experiences with homeowners and contractors alike allows Carmen to provide first-hand knowledge on the difficulties and problems every homeowner and contractor face.

QUICK ORDER FORM

TELEPHONE ORDERS: Call 586-791-3998 Have your credit card ready.

ONLINE ORDERS: www.how-to-hire.com

MAIL ORDERS: LWP Publishing, P.O. Box 66215
Roseville, MI 48066-3795, USA

FAX ORDERS: 586-791-2940. Fax this completed form

PAYMENT METHOD: Check or Money Order (No COD)
Make checks payable to LWP Publishing

Please charge to (check one): ☐ Visa ☐ Master Card

Card #: ☐☐☐☐☐☐☐☐☐☐☐☐☐☐☐☐

Expiration Date: ☐☐ ☐☐

Signature Required: _____

PLEASE SEND MORE FREE INFORMATION ON:

☐ Other Books ☐ Speaking/Seminars ☐ Consulting

NAME: _____

ADDRESS: _____

CITY: _____ **STATE:** _____ **ZIP:** _____

TELEPHONE: _____ **FAX:** _____

E-MAIL ADDRESS: _____

SHIPPING ADDRESS (IF DIFFERENT FROM ABOVE):

SHIP TO NAME: _____

ADDRESS: _____

CITY: _____ **STATE:** _____ **ZIP:** _____

	QUANTITY	PRICE/BOOK	TOTAL
		$19.95	
6% MI TAX			
SHIPPING			
		TOTAL:	

Please add 6% sales tax for products shipped to Michigan addresses.
SHIPPING: U.S.: $4.00 for first book and $2.00 for each additional; International: $9.00 for first book; $5.00 for each additional (estimate).